ARTS
OF
POWER

Statecraft and
Diplomacy

CHAS. W. FREEMAN, JR.

UNITED STATES INSTITUTE OF PEACE PRESS
Washington, D.C.

UNITED STATES INSTITUTE OF PEACE
1200 17th Street NW, Suite 200
Washington, DC 20036-3011

First published 1997
Fifth printing 2005

Printed in the United States of America

The paper used in this publication meets the minimum requirements of American National Standard for Information Sciences—Permanence of Paper for Printed Library Materials, ANSI Z39.48-1984.

Library of Congress Cataloging-in-Publication Data
Freeman, Charles W.
    Arts of power: statecraft and diplomacy / Chas. W. Freeman, Jr.
      p. cm.
    Includes index.
    ISBN 1-878379-65-8 (pbk.)
    1. Diplomacy. 2. International Relations. I. Title.
JX1664.F75 1997   97-3709
327.2—dc21   CIP

CONTENTS

FOREWORD

In the late seventeenth and the eighteenth century, the so-called Westphalian system of international relations was created through a series of peace treaties among major European powers. Shortly after the signing of these treaties a spate of books appeared in Europe on how to do diplomacy. Written by practitioners of the day, and intended in part as manuals for aspiring diplomats, these works signaled the advent of not just a new international system but also a new profession—diplomacy.

The intense political interdependence of the then-new European state system necessitated constant negotiation, and the diplomat became the professional entrusted with management of the system. The greater and lesser European powers established permanent embassies at one anothers' courts and capitals, staffed them with a growing corps of men who made their careers in what soon would be known as diplomatic service, and articulated principles and practices that in many cases still characterize the profession of the diplomat today.

Some of the works written three centuries ago continue to appear on the syllabi of today's foreign service institutes as guides for the young men and women who embark on careers as professional diplomats. The durability of these books is only partly explained by their quality; it is also a reflection of a surprising absence of modern works on the practice of diplomacy. With a few distinguished exceptions, including Harold Nicolson's classic *Diplomacy* and the collection of portraits edited by Gordon Craig and Alexander George entitled *The*

Diplomats, recent practitioners have not attempted to update the classic texts. This is unfortunate, especially because in recent years the conditions that structure diplomatic practice have changed greatly. There has long been need for an updated manual on the practice of statecraft by diplomats.

Ambassador Chas. W. Freeman, Jr.'s *Arts of Power* admirably fills this gap in the professional literature. The author draws on decades of personal experience in the U.S. Foreign Service. His missions in Africa, Asia, and the Middle East have provided him with unusual breadth of vision, and the lessons he has distilled from this experience go far beyond an American perspective. Always seeking the broad conceptual formulation, Freeman has encapsulated much accumulated wisdom into his contemporary analysis of the profession of statecraft.

An assiduous researcher, Freeman first assembled a large collection of observations about statecraft expressed by professionals in the practice of power from many cultures throughout the ages. Organized in dictionary form, these became a companion volume to the present work, recently published in a revised edition by the United States Institute of Peace as *The Diplomat's Dictionary.* Freeman now has distilled that compendium into a series of pithy, acute statements about the various facets of the diplomat's work.

Writing in a tradition that goes back to Hobbes and Locke, one that is reminiscent in places of Machiavelli's advice to princes, the author establishes his definitions and proceeds to apply them to the problems encountered by the modern practitioner of the arts of statecraft. The result is an arresting volume that illuminates the principles and uses of power that shape international relations today. *Arts of Power* will be of prime interest to practitioners of diplomacy and to readers who want a sense of what it's like to represent the interests of a major power in today's world.

Arts of Power also represents a significant contribution to the Institute's ongoing Cross-Cultural Negotiations project. Like *The Diplomat's Dictionary,* this book should be of particular utility to those called upon to serve as mediator, negotiator, governmental envoy, consul, or ambassador—anyone who may be called upon to deal with complex and challenging situations in cross-cultural circumstances.

Arts of Power also complements Raymond Cohen's book *Negotiating Across Cultures,* to appear this year in a revised edition from the Institute of Peace Press—and forthcoming country studies of negotiating behavior in Russia, Japan, and North Korea. These volumes reflect the Institute's continuing attention to research and training on cross-cultural negotiating skills—an issue whose currency can only increase as the twentieth-century age of ideological clashes gives way to the more complex encounters across cultures that characterize the post–Cold War world.

The Chas. Freeman volume, together with other works from the Institute Press, will significantly enhance our understanding of how to build bridges across cultural divides, and thus minimize the mutual incomprehension that often lies behind or fuels violent conflicts.

Richard H. Solomon, President
United States Institute of Peace

PREFACE

The art of statecraft and the craft of diplomacy are as old as human civilization. Statecraft is concerned with the application of the power of the state to other states and peoples. Diplomacy applies this power by persuasive measures short of war.

War, which has been much studied by its practitioners, is an element of statecraft. As Sunzi, one of the earliest and greatest students of the art of war, pointed out millennia ago, however, "weapons . . . are not the tools of the enlightened." He stressed that "to win without fighting is best." Through the ages, enlightened statecraft has viewed the resort to force as an exceptional means rather than the normal way by which to attain its ends. Statecraft has preferred the arts of peace to those of war. It recognizes that there are many tools other than weapons with which to change men's minds.

Generals and admirals understand that the fundamental principles of war, like campaign plans, seldom leave the battlefield unwounded by contact with the enemy. Military commanders nonetheless find inspiration in books of professional maxims as they ponder strategy and tactics by which to prevail in combat. From the time of Sunzi, many members of the military profession have attempted to set down the essentials of the art of war for the edification of commanders and as a stimulus to planning by them.

When I entered the profession of diplomacy, I naturally began to look for something similar on international statecraft and diplomacy, directed at statesmen and diplomats. I did not find it. There are, to be sure, a number of renowned works on the practice of statecraft, such as the Chinese classics, the *Arthas-astra* of Kautilya, the didactic sections of the *Shah Nameh*, Nizam al-Mulk Tusi's *Siyasat-Namah*, and Machiavelli's *The Prince*, that deal in part or in passing with the arts of power as they are applied between states. But the focus of these books is the art of government, or rulership, not international relations. Similarly, there are many works on the practice of diplomacy, dating from the rise of modern diplomacy half a millennium ago. But few of these books attempt to state principles, and fewer still to relate diplomacy to the power of the state it serves. Unlike the modern professions of the law and military science, diplomacy has not developed a case method of instruction. Nor has it matched other professions in the effort to derive principles from cases.

In these circumstances, practitioners of statecraft and diplomacy have been left with a choice between deriving inspiration from their own studies of history or questing for it in academic theories about international relations. (Such theories, while interesting in their own right, are generally so far removed from the world of practitioners as to offer little, if any, stimulus to problem solving.) Yet it is not unreasonable to believe that statesmen and diplomats, like generals and admirals, might—as they make decisions—benefit from a handy means of revisiting the fundamental principles of the arts of power they practice.

The Diplomat's Dictionary, revised and republished by the United States Institute of Peace Press in 1997, was an effort to collect the lore of these arts of power. It may be read, in a sense, as the footnotes to this volume. *The Diplomat's Dictionary* cited observations by practitioners of statecraft and diplomacy in ancient India, China, Greece, and Rome, the Islamic world, and modern Europe, Asia, Africa, and the Americas, as well as my own observations from professional experience. This book distills those observations and restates them in short essays. They may be read separately or as a whole.

I wrote *Arts of Power* during a year as a senior fellow at the United States Institute of Peace. I am very grateful to the Institute for that year. I also very much appreciate its willingness to publish this work. What I have written does not in any way purport to represent the views of the United States Institute of Peace. The writing of *Arts of Power* was very much an individual effort, with all the limitations and opportunities for oversights, errors, and omissions that such an effort implies. I hope for the assistance of readers in improving subsequent editions, if there is a demand for them.

ARTS OF POWER

INTRODUCTION

S tates are established to protect the interests and realize the aspirations of those who create them. To these ends, states compete or cooperate with each other. How well they do this determines whether they rise or fall in wealth and power, and whether they pass their days in tranquility or in turmoil. Statecraft translates national interests and concerns into national goals and strategies. It accumulates and applies the power of the state to other states and peoples to achieve these goals and strategies. Statecraft is the strategy of power.

Power is the capacity to direct the decisions and actions of others. Power derives from strength and will. Strength comes from the transformation of resources into capabilities. Will infuses objectives with resolve. Strategy marshals capabilities and brings them to bear with precision. Statecraft seeks through strategy to magnify the mass, relevance, impact, and irresistibility of power. It guides the ways the state deploys and applies its power abroad. These ways embrace the arts of war, espionage, and diplomacy. The practitioners of these three arts are the paladins of statecraft. They provide statesmen—the men and women who practice statecraft—with their reach and impact abroad.

The military are the fists of statecraft. War is the ultimate argument of the state. The profession of arms applies violence to intimidate and dominate the decisions of other states and peoples.

Espionage is the sixth sense of the state. Spies are statecraft's hidden eyes, ears, and hands. Spymasters serve statesmen by collecting intelligence and by carrying out their directives in secret. Analysts serve statesmen by relating information to national interests.

Diplomacy is the profession of persuasion. Diplomats are statecraft's visible eyes, ears, and hands. They are the voice of their state in foreign lands. They are the peaceable heralds of its power. Statesmen use diplomats to apply this power through overt measures short of war.

To advance national interests, statesmen must discern the hierarchy of such interests and invoke the values that give them force. To build national well-being, preserve domestic tranquility, and ensure freedom from coercion by other states, statesmen must accumulate power for their state. To do this, they must master the elements of power and the means by which it can be applied. To magnify power's effects, statesmen must be able to maneuver their state into positions of strategic advantage. To apply power to other states and peoples, they must be able to use warriors, spies, and diplomats with skill.

Diplomacy is the form that statecraft takes in times of peace. It is the elegantly unbloody arm of strategy in war.

Diplomats work alongside spies and warriors to counsel statesmen and to monitor and guard the interests of their state in relation to others. They harness the power of other states to that of their own in coalitions to promote these interests. They shape the perceptions and actions of other states and peoples. Diplomats contain rivalry between states, harmonize their interests, and build cooperation between them. They erect and operate the framework for their nation's political, economic, cultural, and military interaction with foreigners. Diplomats assist their fellow citizens in international trade, investment, and cultural exchange. They protect the interests of their compatriots abroad.

The task of diplomats is the nonviolent advancement of the political, economic, cultural, and military interests of their state and people. They nurture relations with foreign states that will evoke cooperation or neutrality when war becomes necessary. Diplomats conduct the passage from protest to menace, from dialogue to negotiation, from ultimatum to reprisal, from war to settlement and reconciliation with other states. They build and tend the coalitions that deter or make war. Diplomats disrupt the alliances of enemies and sustain the passivity of potentially hostile powers. Their activity marks the phase of policy prior to war; it aggregates the power of allies; it helps to set the aims of war; it contrives war's termination; it forms, strengthens, and sustains the peace.

The work of diplomats is thus of vital importance to the wealth, power, and well-being of the nation they serve. Like the arts of war and espionage, diplomacy is a path to safety or to ruin that warrants systematic inquiry by statesmen.

THE POWER OF THE STATE

National Interests and National Concerns

S tates are bodies politic. They are manifested in governments controlling a defined territory. States are established to protect the interests and realize the aspirations of those who create them. Governments exist to sustain a people's sovereign independence and to promote its welfare and tranquility. National interests are the relationships a government perceives to exist between these purposes and the wealth and power of other states. The national interests of a state constitute a hierarchy of imperatives guiding its decisions and actions in the international arena.

States wax and wane, coalesce, and cleave asunder. As change proceeds, the national interests of a state conflict or coincide in varying degrees with those of other states. Relations between states, even those closest to each other in culture and temperament, are at once competitive and cooperative. States compete or cooperate to secure territory, strategic advantage, resources, economic privilege, deference, prestige, influence, and ideological ascendancy.

Supreme Interest

The survival of the state and the polity that gave birth to it are by definition a matter of overriding concern to it. A state will defend its continued independent existence at the cost of all other interests and with every means and resource at its disposal. A people will defend its cultural and ethnic identity at

9

the expense of much else. Survival is the *supreme national interest*. Challenges to it lead to war.

Vital Interests

Some matters and developments do not threaten a state's survival but nevertheless bear immediately on its *vital interests*: security, well-being, and domestic tranquility. They are termed "vital" because they touch on the very purposes for which a state is established and maintained by its people. A state will sacrifice many lesser interests and risk suffering heavy damage in war to secure its vital interests if it calculates that it can do so without unduly jeopardizing its supreme interest in survival.

The vital interests of a state include the defense of national unity behind secure frontiers, the securing of strategic advantage and its denial to potential enemies, access to resources essential to national power and well-being, immunity from intimidation, and freedom from subversion or intervention in its internal affairs by other states. A state can be expected to have a sense of urgency about thwarting threats to such vital interests and about seizing opportunities to advance them, using both its diplomats and its warriors to do so. This is the principal inspiration of *reason of state*.

Strategic Interests

Strategic interests arise from matters and developments that do not bear immediately on a state's security, well-being, and domestic tranquility but that have the potential, if left unattended, to directly affect these vital interests or the capacity to advance or defend them. If a state is to prosper, its policies and relationships must be adjusted to address such strategic trends and to bend them to its greatest advantage or least disadvantage. This requirement defines a state's strategic interests.

Such strategic interests include those arising from the strengthening or weakening of adversaries and allies; shifting international alignments and patterns of influence; the discovery of new resources and technologies; changes in the international state system and in regulatory regimes established under it; the emergence of new patterns of economic development and trade, as well as of new doctrines and ideologies; and challenges to the status and treatment of citizens and their property abroad. A state has a strategic interest, in particular, in the maintenance of an international order and state system favoring its continued independence, its capacity to cooperate with other states in addressing matters of common concern, and its ability to effectively promote and defend the broad range of its national interests. This is the source of *reason of system*.

Statesmanship lies in alertness to trends of strategic significance and in the prudent crafting of policies to take advantage of such trends or to offset and mitigate their adverse effects. Such policies may involve military movements, demonstrations, and operations other than war, but seldom entail armed conflict. On the contrary, a state will usually find persuasive diplomacy, rather than coercion or the use of force, to be the least costly means of bringing its power to bear on matters engaging its strategic interests.

Tactical Interests

Many disputes arise in apparently disconnected fashion to affect particular interests of state institutions or private parties. These disputes pose a tactical challenge to a state and its government. If they are not handled well, respect for a state's capacity to fulfill the purposes for which it was established will erode. Its government will fall into disrepute. The behavior at issue may evolve into a pattern, engaging strategic interests and requiring broader and more costly action later. Such cases and controversies, though limited in their immediate impact, may therefore justify firm action by a state to ensure appropriate foreign respect for its stake in their outcome.

Tactical interests emerge from the entire range of activities by a state and its nationals beyond its borders. They include, for example, instances of deviation from internationally or bilaterally accepted norms applying to trade, finance, travel, and other activities of individual enterprises or citizens abroad; foreign respect for national laws, institutions, and frontiers; the international operation of ships and aircraft; the status of diplomats, military officers, and state property; communication between governments and peoples; or due deference to national sovereignty or dignity.

Defense of such interests is the stuff from which the routine of diplomacy is woven.

National Concerns

A people's norms define its national culture and identity. They constitute the canon of *national values* by which a nation judges what is right or wrong and what is decent or abhorrent. A society's values find expression in its *national ideology*. This ideology shapes its international aspirations and inspires the national interests its state is charged with promoting and defending. Ideology combines with interests to generate *national concerns*. These focus and sustain national attention. The values championed by ideology charge interests with emotion and animate national will. Values thus determine the fervor with which interests are pursued. Statesmen must therefore invoke values to inspire national concerns that can sustain policies directed at advancing or defending the interests of their state.

Values remain distinct from interests. A nation's adherence to its values through right conduct is, however, essential to its domestic harmony and important to its sense of well-being. The maintenance of domestic harmony and well-being is a matter of strategic interest to any state. Regard by others for its values also enhances a nation's self-esteem. States therefore often try to promote the spread of their ideology to other peoples, much as individuals attempt to persuade others to embrace their personal beliefs. States do so to vindicate their convictions and to aggrandize their moral leadership, for domestic political reasons and out of other important impulses.

These impulses often find expression in the faith of a state that the expansion of moral consensus will extend the sense of community and the peace its people enjoy at home to other states and peoples. The assumption is that the universal embrace of a common dogma will eliminate sources of international conflict and promote disinterested cooperation between states. Yet history provides little support for this theory and much evidence to the contrary.

Cultural or ideological kinship may ease communication between states. The existence of shared values can reduce mutual misperception and misunderstanding. A common ideology does not create common interests, but it makes it easier for such interests to be discovered and exploited to mutual benefit. It tempers the likelihood that disputes will lead to war. Shared values do not eliminate conflicts of interest, but they facilitate negotiated solutions to them. Shared values and common interests may combine to create a coincidence of national concerns among states. The existence of such shared concerns provides a powerful emotional underpinning for joint or coordinated action in pursuit of the interests to which they are linked.

Yet, shared ideology and values alone seldom provide a basis for joint action. Interests have measurable consequences; they evoke concrete sacrifices by states and coalitions. Values are moral abstractions. States will sacrifice much to defend their national values and ideology against perceived assaults by others. Unless the linkage to national interests is clear, however, states will seldom join with others in taking the offensive to impose their values abroad. If they do, states are seldom able to sustain their commitment beyond the level justified by their interests.

A foreign policy based mainly on the impulse to propagate principles and ideas is, in fact, more disruptive of international order and more likely to generate armed conflict than one based on realistic accommodation of the interests of antagonists. This is because ideological conviction transforms relations between states into a conflict between moral doctrines and claims, in which seeking compromise is seen as unrighteous or immoral.

13

Policies based on ideology expand the arena of international struggle to include the internal policies, social structures, and legitimacy of foreign states. The lack of respect for diversity implicit in such an approach is inconsistent with the peaceable adjustment of differences among states.

The Demands of Statecraft and Diplomacy

Statesmanship rests on a clear perception of the hierarchy of a state's national interests and the extent to which national values give them force. When interests are not clearly defined and ranked, statecraft is forced into self-wounding confusion and incoherence. Policy then invites challenge, deterrence may fail, and the risk of confrontation by inadvertence rises. The failure to identify and prioritize national interests leaves this vital task to the actions of the adversaries who challenge them.

The statesman must clearly discern the nature and ranking of his opponent's and his own people's national concerns with an issue if he is to devise a strategy for advancing the interests of his own state. This is so because the *balance of national concerns* between antagonists measures the relative importance to each of the matters in contention. The balance of national concerns measures the probable resistance by each side to compromise. It defines the threshold of defiance. It regulates the willingness to negotiate. It establishes both the zone of potential mutual accommodation and the distance each party is likely to be willing to travel to reach it.

The task of diplomats is to translate the vision of the statesman into a framework for harmonizing the competing national interests of the parties without unnecessary resort to force. This means contriving an agreement or modus vivendi favorable to the interests of the diplomats' state but acceptable to the other party. Such arrangements must remain tolerable by others, including states not party to them, until the diplomats' state decides to alter them. To accomplish this, diplomats apply a repertoire of professional techniques, backed by the full range of their nation's power.

NATIONAL POWER

The power of states is measured by their ability to alter and channel the behavior of other states. It rests on their will to apply their national strength and potential in contests with others. A state's estimate of its own power helps decide the degree to which it will insist on its views and take risks to see them prevail. Power itself lies, in the first instance, however, in the mind of opponents. How they appraise the consequences of the choices before them determines how they behave. The manipulation of others' perceptions of national will and potential is therefore a critical element of statecraft. The capacity of a state to have its way with another may ultimately be tested directly in war. Short of war, however, a state's power is what its opponents calculate it to be. Perceived determination may count as heavily as capabilities in this calculus.

National Will

First among the elements of the power of the state is its perceived *propensity to risk* using its capabilities to achieve its ends. Neither military, nor economic, nor political strength, no matter how immense, is much value if adversaries disbelieve it will be applied. A convincing record of applying power is thus a major contributor to power. A reputation for timidity diminishes power. Demonstrated willingness by a state to impose solutions on its problems with other states causes others to think twice before challenging it.

Second is the appraisal opponents make of a nation's *fortitude*—its capacity to maintain unity of effort and to persevere in the face of setbacks and sacrifices. Nothing so weakens the seriousness with which a state is taken as a reputation for factiousness, faintheartedness, and lack of stamina. Conversely, a history of stalwart and unwavering pursuit of clearly defined objectives greatly bolsters the credibility of national power.

Third is the estimate of a state's *obstinacy*—its determination to insist on terms advantageous to it, rather than to rush to compromise. The purpose of international negotiation is not to reach agreement; it is to obtain the acquiescence of others in adjustments in relations that advance national interests. A state that so values harmony and detests discord that it strives for agreement as an end in itself devalues its power.

Fourth is the specific nature of the issues in dispute and their place in the *hierarchy of national interests* of the contending parties. The supreme interest of a state is its survival as an independent polity. A state's vital interests lie in the preservation of the territory, wealth, and domestic tranquility and the other advantages history and effort have brought its people. The closer an issue seems to lie to its supreme or vital interests, the more intensely concerned a state will be, and the less likely it will be to yield. The relative intensity of concern about the interests at stake in a controversy measures a *balance of fervor* between the parties to a dispute. This balance determines the risks each will take. It regulates the effort each will make to mobilize its national potential to realize its own ambitions or to thwart the ambitions of the other.

Fifth is the extent to which a state enjoys a reputation for well-informed, bold, and shrewd *decision making* by its government and national elites. The belief that an opponent may be able to anticipate and counter one's maneuvers is a constraint on action. The presumption that a state will defend its interests vigorously, and in ways that are difficult to anticipate, deters challenges to them.

National Strengths

Political strength is measured in the ability of a state to persuade others of the wisdom of its policies, to unite them in its

16

purposes, and to inspire them to subordinate their own interests to its own. It is a product of national vitality and unity as well as of the prestige born of size, cultural distinction, economic and military strength, and perceived potential.

Political strength is magnified by coalition and the widest possible network of cooperative international relationships. It is manifested in the extent of a state's diplomatic and other representation abroad. Political strength is more effective as an inducement for cooperation than as an instrument of chastisement. It is the basis for most diplomacy.

Cultural strength is seen in the ability of a nation to inspire other nations to emulate its ideas, admire its achievements, and use its language. Cultural diplomacy is the projection abroad—in the form of prestige—of moral, intellectual, scientific, artistic, and cultural achievement at home. Such prestige enhances the attentiveness and raises the receptivity of foreigners to proposals from those possessing it. It thereby adds weight to a state's political, economic, and military strengths.

Cultural strength is built through direct contacts between peoples, institutions, and individuals, with or without state sponsorship. It is enhanced by interaction and dissipated by nonintercourse. It is a prerequisite for effective propaganda but not an instrument of coercion that can be applied to specific issues.

Economic strength is measured in a nation's financial assets, output of goods and services, and market. It finds expression in reliance by other nations on access to that nation's capital, output, and market. It is manifested in a state's trade and investment flows to and from other nations.

By contrast with military prowess, economic strength is built through the widest possible pattern of interdependence with other states. Its influence depends on the presence of banks, businesses, and businesspeople abroad and a comparable foreign presence at home.

Coercive economic measures can be applied to other nations to the extent that a nation is willing to forgo or arrange substitutes for the goods, services, and capital it exchanges with those nations. The purpose of such measures is to secure advantages for national exports of goods, services, and capital or to add an element of economic compulsion to political demands. Their effectiveness is multiplied by coalition and cooperation with other states. Their efficacy is greatest when it is sharply focused to achieve economic rather than political objectives. The impact of economic measures is difficult to predict and slow to register on an adversary. Threats to employ economic measures are usually more effective than their actual use.

Military strength is the most unilateral element of national power. It is also the most costly in treasure and in blood. Military strength provides the most immediate and brutal means by which national power may be brought to bear on other states. It is measured in warfighting skills. These skills are the product of recruitment, training, discipline, equipment, logistics, and command.

The logic of military strength is intimidation, death, and destruction. The purpose of its use is to compel the acceptance of demands to which an enemy would not otherwise submit. Its function is to demonstrate that submission to the terms demanded is the enemy's wisest and least costly choice.

Military strength is greatest when it is self-sufficient and can be brought to bear unilaterally. It is independently developed through sustained national effort. It can be augmented by alliances and the availability of auxiliaries, but dependence on these augmentations reduces its capacity to intimidate.

National Potential

The capacity of a state actually to apply its political, economic, and military capabilities to other states on an issue determines its national potential with regard to that issue. The *balance of capabilities* of the contending parties decides the outcome if both are equally determined.

Capabilities are capacities for action to reward or punish other states. They may be military, economic, political, or cultural. Capabilities are influence with observable consequences. They vary in mass, relevance, impact, irresistibility, and sustainability.

The *mass* of a capability is measured by its preponderance and concentration. Mass determines the capacity of a state to dominate an arena of contention. Military mass consists of a concentration of forces capable of overwhelming the opposition. Economic mass is measured by the degree of monopoly in the supply or demand for specific goods and services. Political mass consists of dominant persuasiveness. Cultural mass is represented by intellectual preeminence.

The *relevance* of a capability is determined by the degree to which it can be brought to bear on the issues in dispute. Those capabilities that, for whatever reason, cannot be applied to an opponent to influence the resolution of a particular issue are irrelevant to national potential with respect to that issue. Those that do not touch an opponent's interests at stake in a dispute or do not correlate to its decisions on the matters in dispute are either ineffectual or provocative, risking a widening and deepening of the dispute. The balance of capabilities between states must therefore be assessed by reference to capabilities and vulnerabilities bearing on the specific issues between them. This balance cannot be assessed in general or abstract terms. Large states may be bested by much smaller states on specific issues when the balance of relevant capabilities favors the smaller.

The degree to which an opponent feels an injury or inducement applied to it through a capability gauges that capability's *impact*. Impact is affected by distance, time, and experience. Nearness, both geographic and psychological, enhances the impact of actions by a state. Distance weakens capabilities; great distance weakens them greatly. With time and experience, what was once seen as intolerable may come to be suffered with equanimity. What was once seen as highly desirable may come to be taken for granted.

A capability may be vulnerable to devaluation through countermeasures or to elimination through reprisal. It may be frustrated by evasion or the development of means to offset its effects. The extent to which a capability cannot be countered or offset measures its *irresistibility*.

The expenditure of time and national effort works to reinforce capabilities or to exhaust them, determining their *sustainability*.

The *national potential* of a state rests on the mass, relevance, impact, irresistibility, and sustainability of its existing politico-economic and military capabilities and on the quantity and quality of the human and natural resources available to enhance and expand these capabilities. The extent to which national potential can be realized reflects the organizational, industrial, and technological proficiency of a society. National potential is ultimately determined, however, by the degree to which a society's political system allows its state to concentrate and apply national skills and resources quickly in a struggle.

National potential also reflects the strategic attributes of a state's national territories and footholds abroad. National potential is enhanced by a state's ability to rally powerful allies and auxiliaries, joining the strength of others to its cause. It is weakened by isolation or association with the weak and the vulnerable. These factors help determine the extent to which a state can apply its strengths to counter and reduce the national potential of an opponent, compelling that opponent to yield and accommodate it.

National Power

Statecraft rests on accurate appraisal of the power of one's own nation and its allies in relation to the power of rivals. It consists of strategy directing actions to affect this balance of power and to make use of national strengths to advance national interests.

Power is the capacity to control the course of events, including the decisions and actions of others. The joining of will to strength and potential produces power. In politics, however, perceptions are reality. In diplomacy, perceived power is real power. The *balance of perceived power* between states decides the outcome of struggles short of war. Only in war is the true *balance of power* between opponents tested and determined. Even in war, mutual perceptions shape the decisions and therefore the actions of the combatants.

The calculus of statesmen therefore begins with an accurate assessment of both the power of their own nation and the power opponents perceive their state to have with regard to the specific matters in dispute. This calculus then reckons the actual power of opponents and their perceptions of their own power. It includes comparable estimates for the allies and auxiliaries of both sides. This is the foundation upon which sound strategy is formulated.

It is, however, not enough for statesmen merely to assess the balance of perceived power and of power itself. They must act to enhance both. They thereby expand their options for strategy. Perceptions of the elements of power by opponents can be manipulated. Both will and capabilities can be demonstrated for effect. Leadership can fortify resolve. Government can muster national potential to strengthen capabilities. Strategy must unite national will with national strength and potential to bring power to bear effectively on other states. The accumulation and effective application of power are the central tasks of statecraft.

INTELLIGENCE, ESPIONAGE, AND COVERT OPERATIONS

Intelligence is knowledge that is relevant to statecraft. Timely insight into the intentions, as well as the capabilities, of other states is essential to defend and advance the national interests of the state in peace as well as in war. Such insight is gained through the collection of information. Information becomes intelligence when it is analyzed in light of national interests and objectives.

To fail to give adequate attention to the collection of intelligence is to gamble with the fate of the nation. There are two main sources of intelligence: overt collection through the news media, scholarly writing, and diplomatic reporting; and clandestine collection through espionage.

Journalists, scholars, and diplomats (including military attachés) collect information openly from those who volunteer it. To some degree, states can control the access to information of such openly avowed information collectors, and shape their understanding of events. To that extent, states can manipulate the perceptions of public and expert opinion as well as those of governments.

Spies, by contrast, collect information that others seek to withhold or conceal. They seek to gain access to information in ways that cannot be observed, controlled, manipulated, or prevented by those from whom they gain it. Their work is a vitally important supplement to that of open collectors of information. Organizations and capabilities developed for espionage also provide the state with the means to act in anonymity internationally.

23

Journalism

Information reported by the news media is timely but often superficial and incomplete. It focuses on current, visible events and is hastily composed to catch and briefly hold the attention of an idle and largely uninformed audience. It is therefore fragmentary and anecdotal rather than comprehensive and analytical. Its point of reference is novelty rather than the relationship of events or information to the national interest.

Those who speak to journalists know that what they disclose will be made public in one way or another, often in unexpected contexts or dramatic ways. Only the naive fail to speak guardedly or calculatedly to the press, weighing the impact of their words on public opinion at home or abroad. People cooperate with journalists to state their organization's view, to advance a cause they espouse, or simply to aggrandize themselves. They may anonymously embarrass political adversaries, discredit policies to which they object, or divert attention from themselves or matters under their purview.

Journalists are not accountable to their audience for the accuracy of what they report. They seldom comment critically on one another's reporting. Journalists seek out what is new, not what is relevant to decisions by statesmen. Information in the news media is usually more evocative than reliable. It sets the public context for policy decisions but is an inadequate basis for making them.

Scholarship

Scholarship is usually reliable but hardly ever timely. Scholars delve deeply into subjects, supplementing or refuting information drawn from the news media with their own investigative insights. They write for their peers, who are quick to call attention to their inaccuracies or inadequate documentation of facts. They are, however, often narrowly focused within a single discipline and intent on proving a thesis, theory, or methodology. Their perspectives and the subjects they research are therefore seldom congruent with the practical issues and decisions before policymakers. The writings of scholars nonetheless yield much useful background information and delineate the context within which to interpret current information from other sources.

Diplomatic Reporting and Analysis

Diplomatic reporting focuses on national interests and can be timely and topical. An efficient national security policy apparatus will ensure that it addresses the questions actually before policymakers. Its accuracy and completeness will be systematically evaluated by the government to which it is directed. At its best, diplomatic reporting points to the implications for national interests of the personalities, perspectives, reasoning, motivations, objectives, and actions of foreign decision makers. It combines confidential interviews with foreign decision makers and elites with information drawn from scholarly writings and media reporting, as well as corroborative information from espionage.

Since diplomatic reporting is confidential, its sources have less fear of exposure than they do when talking to journalists, and they may speak considerably more candidly. Sources can be identified in reports without being compromised. The motives of such sources for their apparent indiscretions can be analyzed. Nevertheless, those who speak with diplomats (including military attachés) are always aware that their words will reach the government the diplomats represent. They may therefore speak cautiously and for effect. This is especially so if they have reason to doubt an embassy's discretion, if its capital has a reputation for leaking information to the press, or if its codes are thought to be less than completely secure.

Like journalism and scholarship, diplomatic reporting draws on multiple sources. Unlike them, however, it is subject to critique by peers as it is written. If produced by a well-run embassy staffed by competent, professional diplomats, it can provide a reliable flow of essential information for those who must make decisions in its nation's capital.

Espionage

Those states and societies that are most reluctant to reveal information and that seek most strenuously to control it invite the greatest efforts at foreign information collection. The clandestine collection of information therefore finds its greatest utility where it is most resisted. The object of espionage, like that of diplomatic reporting, is insight into the military and economic capabilities of foreign states and the political intentions of those who lead them. Capabilities can be enumerated and evaluated. Actions can be observed and depicted. Words may be overheard or read. Thoughts can be captured only by agents who are privy to them.

Weapons can be counted and described. Their quality can be appraised by watching them in use. Military exercises can be seen and heard. The leadership, command, control, logistical support, and warfighting competence of the forces conducting them can be evaluated. Economic prowess can be measured in statistics. Economic points of vulnerability can be identified by analysis. So can political relationships and pressure points. For information about capabilities, overt collection by diplomats, scholars, and journalists is usually the primary source, though usefully supplemented by clandestine collection by spies and their devices.

Spies and Devices

What is spoken aloud among foreign decision makers is not easily overheard and recorded. What they write to one another is difficult to intercept and reproduce. What they intend is still less easily ascertained. Spies and their devices are usually the primary source of intelligence about intentions. Spies are undeclared and undeparted defectors from the nation and cause they pretend to continue to serve—hidden traitors to their own state and unheralded heroes to another. They are the concealed eyes and ears of statesmen in foreign lands.

Spies have many motivations for taking up their awkward role. They may volunteer out of conviction born of disaffection from their own government and attraction to what they imagine to be a morally superior one, the need to give an empty life spiritual significance, or the desire to gain security or advantages for themselves and their families in an eventual life abroad. They may be susceptible to appeals to their greed for wealth or lust for power, or to the arousal of fears that misconduct or indecent behavior in which they have engaged (or have been entrapped) will be exposed. Spies motivated by conviction are generally more reliable than those responding to baser instincts.

Devices, including those that secretly record images, signals, and sounds, provide information unfiltered by human frailty. Information gleaned through such devices is not easily blocked or controlled by foreign counterintelligence efforts. The development and use of such devices is a principal task of intelligence services. Some devices work at a distance. Others, however, must be hidden or employed on site. Spies are as essential to placing and operating these devices as they are for overhearing what devices cannot overhear and reading what machines cannot read. Only human agents can elicit direct information about the intentions of those in authority.

Intelligence Officers

Intelligence officers are usually spymasters rather than spies themselves. Normally, that role is better played by natives of the target state. Intelligence officers may be civilian or military. They are charged with identifying potential agents and then recruiting, training, equipping, directing, counseling, and sustaining them as spies while protecting their identity from inadvertent disclosure. Intelligence officers may be part of an embassy, consulate, or other official presence, or they may appear to be entirely unaffiliated with a foreign government. They may work under a false identity or flag. A false identity allows intelligence officers to operate more freely than an official one, though at greater risk should they be discovered. A false flag allows them to enlist agents who sympathize with the state they pretend to work for but who are unsympathetic to the one they actually serve.

Intelligence officers normally carry out the functions appropriate to their apparent status part of the time, while devoting other hours to the management of espionage. Some intelligence officers assigned abroad may, however, be identified to the state in which they work. Intelligence liaison is an important adjunct to diplomatic relations. Official relations between intelligence agencies allow states to exchange intelligence, to arrange support for mutually beneficial intelligence collection efforts, or to mount joint operations. Contact between intelligence services also provides each of them with obvious opportunities for the recruitment of spies in the ranks of the other. Intelligence liaison must therefore be handled with caution by the parties to it.

Intelligence relations may be open, as through the exchange of military attachés, or concealed from all but those with a need to know. When intelligence relations are open, they are an element in diplomatic relations. Intelligence officers, including military attachés, act in a diplomatic capacity when conducting liaison with their foreign counterparts. Their reporting and analysis are similar to those of diplomats, though communicated in nondiplomatic channels. In addition to the flow of information and insights they gain, liaison officers are, like diplomats, in a position to convey official views and to influence the policies of the state to which they are accredited. When intelligence relations are concealed, they may survive a public break in diplomatic relations and provide a temporary substitute for them as a means of official communication.

Intelligence Analysis

To become intelligence useful to decision makers, information from all sources must be collated, analyzed, and then summarized in the form of judgments about the likely course of future events. Gaps in information must be identified so that they can be filled by further overt or clandestine collection. This essentially scholarly task is best done by specialists in the national capital who are involved in neither intelligence collection nor policy formulation. Separation of analysis from collection reduces the risk of overreliance on a particular source of information. Separation of analysis from policy formulation helps to reduce bias in favor of particular policy options before the statesman. Analysts are charged with describing, explaining, and predicting trends and events. Statecraft demands that statesmen not only understand trends and events, but that they seize, shape, and direct them.

Counterintelligence

Even as it conducts espionage against foreign states, a state must protect itself against their efforts to spy on it. A state's counterintelligence activities seek to prevent foreign states from gaining information relevant to hostile statecraft. Counterintelligence measures include the safeguarding and encryption of sensitive information, periodic investigation to ensure the continuing loyalty of those entrusted with it, and the control of access to places where it is located or likely to be discussed. They extend also to the concealment of facilities and activities, the surveillance of foreign officials or suspected intelligence officers, and the use of spies and their devices to unmask the modus operandi, collection priorities, roster of agents, and operations of foreign intelligence services. They embrace the provision of false information through double agents and through covert action by spies and agents of influence.

Covert Action

A state may sometimes find it most effective to act anonymously to promote its interests. It may seek to manipulate the perceptions of foreign governments and publics, to subvert and contrive the overthrow of hostile governments, or to assist insurgents against an enemy or occupation regime without appearing to be doing so. The organizations and capabilities a

29

state has developed for espionage and counterintelligence can serve these purposes as well.

The perceptions and policies of a foreign state may be directly affected by spies who, in addition to collecting information, disseminate it. Some spies are in a position to help shape the policies of a foreign government directly as "agents of influence." Less direct mastery of foreign government decisions may be exercised through the deliberate planting of credible but false information in the form of forged documents, sham reporting by double agents, or misleadingly sourced, counterfeit stories in the news media. Such "gray" and "black" propaganda can have a significant impact on foreign views without implicating the state that originated it.

Democratic states are founded on open competition between their politicians, political parties, interest groups and associations, and news media. These elements of their decision-making process are susceptible to influence by clandestine financial or other aid. The decision-making process of independent states with less open politics are more difficult to penetrate. Such states are, however, susceptible to the planting of false information. They may also be vulnerable to support for individuals or groups that seek or might be induced to carry out the assassination of their leaders or the overthrow of their governments; for example, revolutionaries or the military (through coups d'état). Exile groups may be able to distract and weaken hostile states if given support to mount effective internal opposition and insurgency against their governments. A state's intelligence services can often arrange for the delivery of assistance to rebels in ways that conceal its source or make its origin difficult to prove.

Statesmen should hesitate before engaging in any activity that might bring severe discredit upon them or their state if revealed. The decision to employ covert measures must be weighed against the risk of covert retaliation or embarrassment from public disclosure. Involvement in acts of violence, such as assassination or support for revolutionary destabilization, may invoke retaliation in kind or overt conflict with those against whom the violence is directed. Similarly, the costs of exposure may on occasion outweigh the benefits of success in directly manipulating the decisions of foreign governments. It is a sound maxim of statecraft that no secret is immune from discovery and no action is immune from retaliation.

The Use of Intelligence

Intelligence is the sensory apparatus of the state. It is the means by which the state perceives both threats and opportunities in the international environment. Accurate understanding of that environment is the prerequisite for the survival and prosperity of nations. Intelligence magnifies the mass, relevance, impact, and irresistibility of power by allowing capabilities to be applied with precision. It is the basis of sound calculation in statecraft and diplomacy. There is only one thing more fatal to statesmen than the failure to collect and analyze intelligence: the failure to heed it.

POLITICAL ACTIONS AND MEASURES

Power is the capacity to control events, including the decisions and actions of others. The basis of power is the joining of military, economic, political, or cultural strength and potential with will. Politics is the art of aggregating power and applying it to achieve desired ends. In its international dimension, it rests on the capacity of statesmen to persuade others of the wisdom of their policies, to unite them in common purposes, and to inspire them to subordinate their interests to these purposes.

Political actions are those that add the power of allies, partners, and friends to one's own, or that divide and weaken the power of enemies, opponents, and rivals. *Political measures* are those that apply the persuasive force of power to adjustments in military, economic, political, and cultural relations with other states through measures short of war.

States compete or cooperate to secure territory, strategic advantage, resources, economic benefit, deference, prestige, influence, and ideological ascendancy. It is rare that the power of a single state is sufficient to accomplish these purposes; hence, the need to aggregate the power of many states to gain political mass. A state aggregates power through the cultivation of bilateral relations with other states; the formation of coalition, alliance, and client state relationships; the establishment of protectorates, buffer states, and spheres of influence; participation in international organizations; and propaganda.

Coalitions

When two or more states share latent common political, economic, or military interests, a leader may be able persuade them to recognize the extent to which their interests coincide. The leader may then be able to harness these states to a common design to seize an opportunity or frustrate a threat to such common interests. Perception of opportunity requires uncommon foresight and strategic vision. Less perspicacity is needed to see a threat. Coalitions are more often formed out of fear than from a vision of common gain.

Coalitions come into being to deter others' political, economic, or military plans or actions; to reverse those actions; or to exploit the opportunities they create. Coalitions may have a political, economic, or military focus. Coalition partners should be chosen for the mass they add, the relevance of their capabilities to the task at hand, their lack of vulnerability to countermeasures, and the reliability with which they can be expected to sustain the common effort. Coalitions may be formed ad hoc, in response to sudden developments, or preconcerted under an entente. States seek to join coalitions for many motives: to share the burden of advancing or defending national interests, to court the protection or favor of potential patron states, to gain economic support or military equipment and training, to make money by hiring out their capabilities, to share in the spoils, or to be in a position to profit from the resolution of issues in dispute. Coalitions serve the common denominator of such disparate interests for as long as that common denominator exists. Once a coalition attains its political, economic, or military objective or finds it impossible to achieve, the coalition dissolves, leaving little but nostalgia behind it.

Many rush to the aid of the victor; the allies of the defeated melt away. But victory and defeat are equally fatal to coalitions. As common interests and purposes are realized, separate interests and purposes reassert themselves. If common interests and purposes seem likely to be defeated, each state is tempted to resume its struggle for singular advantage. The sustained management of coalitions is therefore among the most difficult challenges of statecraft and diplomacy.

Alliances

Alliances are coalitions that have been formalized to give them greater solemnity, durability, and salience. They commit the parties to act jointly or in parallel to advance or protect specified common interests. The main advantage of alliance is that it makes a joint response to events by the allies seem more certain. This raises the deterrent value of their association. The highest form of alliance creates collective planning and decision-making bodies and preconcerts procedures by which the allies may implement joint military, economic, and political measures to aid or oppose other states.

Like other forms of coalition, alliances remain alive only as long as the interests that bring them into being persist and seem realizable. The formality of alliances, the jointly operated institutions to which they can give birth, and the habits of cooperation they engender, however, make them awkward to dissolve. Alliances often survive in form long after they have died in substance. Less frequently, new purposes arise to revive and redirect them.

Client States

A larger state may see the survival of a smaller state or the defense of certain of its interests as supportive of its own national interests. It may therefore become the patron and protector of the smaller state, assisting its client militarily, economically, and politically without demanding much, if anything, in return. Such relations are mutually beneficial but do not entail the reciprocal obligations inherent in alliances.

Patron-client relationships contain difficulties for both sides. Dependence on the protection or largesse of a patron may compromise the client state's independence, curtail its freedom of action, or embroil it in controversies remote from its interests. These complications of dependence can ignite nationalist resentment within the client state and destabilize its politics. Nevertheless, the very weakness, vulnerability, and dependence of the client state make its survival and well-being the central, shared concern of the relationship. It can often play on this concern to gain influence over its patron's policies while denying the patron comparable influence over its own. Thus, economic and military weakness may become political strength, and the flea may come to guide the dog. When this happens, the patron state may find itself enmeshed in passionate controversies of no inherent importance to it. Its maneuverability may be constrained, its own interests damaged or put at risk, or its resources subjected to unbearable demands. States should enter patron-client relationships dispassionately and should seek to maintain a clear mutual understanding of their limits.

Protectorates

A larger state may have a vital or strategic interest in the international orientation or domestic tranquility of a smaller state. It may, however, lack confidence in the capacity of that state to survive, to sustain its independence against pressure from others, or to curb domestic disorder that menaces the stability of its neighbors. In such cases, the larger state may decide to establish a protectorate over the smaller state, assuming responsibility for its defense and foreign relations, and exercising a measure of guidance over its domestic affairs. Such an assertion of suzerainty can secure and stabilize an otherwise volatile situation, but it may prove costly. The suzerain's dominance may ignite nationalist sentiment in the protectorate. Both aggrieved domestic parties and hostile outside powers will be tempted to exploit this. The suzerain may find itself compelled to spend increasing amounts of money to buy the complacency, if not the loyalty, of the people of its protectorate. It may periodically find it necessary to use its armed forces to subdue a restive populace. These economic and military imperatives can become a serious diversion of the suzerain state's resources and energy.

Buffer States

A state may have an interest in denying strategic use of an adjacent territory to a rival state but may be reluctant or too weak to assert a protectorate over that territory. In such cases, that state may join its rival in a joint guarantee of the independence of the state or states occupying the territory in question and renunciation of military deployments in it. Such a joint guarantee establishes a buffer zone between the rivals and separates their military forces. It reduces the threat of attack by either through the buffer state. Buffer state arrangements are, however, reliable only when there is no imbalance of military power between the rival states and their potential coalition partners. An imbalance will tempt the stronger state to violate the territory of the buffer in the event of war with its weaker rival. By doing so, it may gain the advantage of surprise, while keeping combat operations at a remove from its own territory.

Spheres of Influence

A large, powerful state may seek to exclude potential adversaries from gaining military, economic, political, or cultural advantages or influence in a region of special strategic interest to it or in which it has traditionally exercised dominion. To this end, it may forbid actions by other states in that region. If the hegemon's national power is sufficient to back its claim, it can establish the region as its sphere of influence, preserving its advantages and inhibiting competition from other states there. The states and peoples within its sphere of influence are likely, however, to resent constraints on their freedom of international maneuver. The forces of change in the region will regard the hegemon as an enemy. Revolutions and reform movements, even those with which the hegemon sympathizes, will see the hegemon's enemies as natural sources of support. Resentment of a sphere of influence by those included in it may therefore stimulate the very inroads by rival states the hegemon had intended to preclude.

International Organizations and Regulatory Regimes

Most states recognize a strategic interest in the maintenance of a stable international order. International law is the constantly evolving code of ethics that summarizes states' expectations of one another and of the international system to which they belong. Common acceptance of custom, usage, and rules of conduct moderates the interaction between states and adds a measure of predictability to their behavior. The advantages they derive from such moderation and predictability inspire states to combine to insist on respect for specific norms of international conduct by those who violate their consensus.

States may also come together to expand the realm of agreement on such norms or to add to them by concluding multilateral compacts and conventions. These facilitate expanded interaction between states and the societies they rule, secure mutual advantages, advance common interests, alleviate common threats, address common dangers, or allow problems to be addressed without invoking national rivalries. International organizations and regulatory regimes can apply agreed principles to the political, economic, cultural, or military interaction between member states. Such international institutions also supply states with forums within which to address disputes touching matters of multilateral concern.

The principal advantages of international organizations are their capacity to make technical services and expertise available to their members, to give voice to consensus, to provide a convenient means of contact between states that are otherwise estranged, to allow verbal argument to substitute for more violent forms of confrontation, to serve as repositories for problems that are not ripe for resolution, and to handle issues while tempering and constraining national rivalries. The main failings of international organizations are their inclusion in decision making of states with no real stake in the decisions they make, their inability to formulate objectives above the lowest common denominator of their members' views, their tendency to paralyze initiative, and their facilitation of inflammatory rhetoric that may harden attitudes rather than promote compromise.

When states or organizations indulge in rhetoric or behavior that is offensive to other states they may expect retribution. This reality ensures that most states are polite to one another and check the worst excesses of their representatives in multilateral organizations. States appraise the interests, policies, and activities of other states and organizations in relation to their own interests. Institutions soon take on a life of their own, but all relations between states, even those conducted in the quasi-parliamentary context of international organizations, are therefore ultimately bilateral. So are relations between states and multilateral organizations. Such organizations, once established, are difficult to abolish, but they can accomplish no more than their members are willing to allow them to accomplish. This limitation is both their reason for being and the source of much of their incapacity.

Political Measures

In peace or in war, states draw on coalitions and alliances—and on the advantages afforded by client states, protectorates, buffer states, spheres of influence, and international organizations—to aggregate power to accomplish the adjustment of their relations with other states. Political measures such as propaganda and negotiation seek to accomplish such adjustments by measures short of war.

Propaganda is political power in the form of psychological manipulation. It draws on a state's cultural strength to persuade foreign elites of the logic, justice, and reasonableness of the state's policies and activities abroad, to enlist their sympathy and support for these policies and actions, and to predispose foreign leaders to facilitate and accommodate them. Propaganda acquires mass by reduction of a message to its simplest arguments and by constant repetition of those arguments. The extent to which propaganda corresponds to the beliefs and perspectives of those it seeks to influence determines its relevance. Delivery of its message through media that reach opinion leaders gives it impact. Its irresistibility is established by the extent to which it can withstand contrary argument. Its sustainability rests on its perceived sincerity and truth; these alone give it credibility that will survive events as they unfold. (This is, of course, not the case with "gray" or "black" propaganda. Such propaganda has a concealed source and many outlets.)

Propaganda eases the path of negotiation but cannot replace negotiation as a means of peaceful adjustments in relations between states. Negotiation is a search for common ground between parties with disparate interests, objectives, and perspectives. To succeed, it must harmonize their interests, prove that their objectives are at least in part compatible, and bring them to see that agreement is preferable to the alternatives. Negotiation is the central task of diplomacy.

CULTURAL INFLUENCE

National culture is the projection abroad—in the form of prestige—of moral, intellectual, scientific, artistic, economic, and cultural achievements at home. The foreign image of a state and its people is an intangible but powerful underpinning of their influence in other states and among other peoples.

Favorable perceptions of a nation's culture enhance its ability to persuade others of the wisdom of its policies and to lead them in directions congenial to its interests. To have studied or lived among another people is to have gained a more nuanced understanding of them and their state. Foreigners who embrace a nation's language establish a bond with its speakers. To know a nation's language is to know something of its soul and to be more open to its ideas. The cultivation of favorable foreign images of the national culture and the propagation of the national language are thus a matter of strategic interest to the state. The devotion of appropriate effort to these tasks is a modest but profitable investment for statecraft.

Culture and language are both the product and the icon of a nation's people. The state may nurture their development and support their transmission abroad, but foreigners can appreciate them best through direct contact with individuals and their ideas, activities, and artifacts. A state concerned with building influence abroad will therefore favor the greatest possible interaction of its citizens with foreigners. The severance of contact with another state and its people immediately reduces influence over them. Over time, it reduces their receptivity to the ideas of those from whom they have become estranged.

41

The Promotion of Language and Culture

Language is the sound of thought: the music of the human intellect. It is the means by which human beings reason and the principal tool they use to communicate with one another. The attractiveness of a language derives from the ideas that it is used to express and the cultural artifacts to which it affords access. Translation can make these ideas and artifacts available, though without full nuance and tone, to those who do not know the language in which they were originally expressed. No one will learn a foreign language that is viewed as the key to an empty room. The effort to propagate a language begins with translation of its ideas into other languages. A state wishing to promote the spread of its language will encourage such translation.

Languages are best learned among their native speakers or from them. A state that welcomes foreign students to its universities and training institutions promotes both its language and its culture. It thereby builds an international constituency of partisans for its ideas. Foreign teachers of language and culture can multiply this constituency in their own lands. A state that encourages the export of its books, visual and performing arts, and broadcast media nurtures this constituency. It also influences its partisans' views of contemporary issues. A state seeking to increase receptivity to its ideas and sympathy for its policies will therefore make the investments necessary to ease foreign access to its language and culture.

Linguistic and Cultural Preeminence

In every age, in every region, there is a nation or group of nations whose language comes to serve as the common medium of diplomatic and other interaction between states and peoples and whose culture inspires emulation by others.

Such preeminence is born of wealth and power, reflected in the intellectual, political, economic, and military prowess of the nation that achieves it. The emergence of cultural and linguistic preeminence is a natural result of empire, the peace of the universal state or an international state system based on feudal contention. Nevertheless, since a common language and standard of decorous behavior are a practical requirement for dealings between states and peoples, they are also a feature of international orders built on pluralist balance.

The conduct of diplomacy and trade in a lingua franca (other than an artificial language or "pidgin") greatly facilitates the international dealings of its native speakers. It eases understanding and acceptance by others of their views. It breaks down barriers to their international business and other activities. The fact that their culture has become the source from which standards of behavior are drawn internationally brings them further advantages. Linguistic and cultural preeminence in a given region or throughout the globe constitutes a position of special influence. It reinforces the capacity of the people who possess it to sway others to their purposes. The international prestige attached to a nation's language and culture is thus a significant element of that nation's power. Its rise boosts a nation's capacity to lead others. Its devaluation accelerates a decline in ease of access and influence abroad.

The prestige of languages and cultures waxes and wanes inexorably with the wealth and power of their homelands. Such change need not, however, proceed apace. The continuing prestige of a nation's language and culture abroad can lend that nation greater eminence and influence, and therefore greater persuasive power, than it otherwise would have, considering its decline in relation to the growing capacities of others. No state can be counted wise that allows such an advantage to wither from neglect.

The Utility of Cultural Exchange

Cultural intercourse with a foreign people is a path to political influence over them. It is also a catalyst for increased economic penetration of their society. A state that inhibits or restricts the export of its own culture to other societies weakens itself in the contest for international influence. An increase in cultural

43

activity abroad builds the power of the state; a decrease diminishes influence.

A state that restricts access to the culture of another state reduces that state's prestige and influence among its citizens. This may be expedient, but it is not without cost. A society walled off from outside stimulus risks its own cultural, economic, and political vigor. The regulation of cultural intercourse with a foreign people is a strategic, not a tactical, instrument of statecraft. The severance of cultural interaction with another society constitutes unilateral disarmament in the duel of policies and ideas.

THE USE OF ECONOMIC MEASURES

National wealth is mainly the output of peoples rather than of the states that govern them. Usually, the state regulates and benefits from, but does not directly conduct, most of the activities that constitute the national economy. Economic prowess is nevertheless a critical element in the power of its state over other peoples and, through them, over their states and governments. Statecraft must draw on economic strength, as it does on other elements of national strength and potential, to carry on a nation's political, economic, and military cooperation and competition with other states.

The extent to which a state can mobilize the resources of its national economy (and the economies of other states) to carry out government functions determines the extent to which it can realize its military, political, and cultural potential. The extraction of economic resources by the state to foster these noneconomic strengths is, however, largely at the expense of economic strength. High levels of taxation and other forms of state interference in an economy may augment national noneconomic power in the short term. In the long term, however, such exactions weaken the base of an economy and therefore degrade national potential. The nurturing of a nation's financial assets, output of goods and services, technological prowess, and domestic and foreign markets is an important strategic task of statecraft that should seldom be sacrificed to tactical concerns.

Economic statecraft is directed at building national economic strength to enhance national well-being and to ensure continued freedom from coercion by other states. The terms by which trade and investment are conducted usually favor one party more than another. To promote national well-being and to build economic strength, the state must concern itself with maximizing profit for its economy by gaining more advantageous terms for transactions with foreign economies. To reduce the danger of foreign coercion, it must strive to diversify the sources and destinations of its nation's imports and exports. such diversification can enable a state to avoid strategic dependence on a single foreign economy or on the economies of states that may collude against it. To gain commanding influence over another state, a state may, conversely, seek to foster such dependence. The desire of states to achieve a favorable economic balance differs little from their desire to achieve a favorable strategic balance.

International commerce consists of reciprocal transactions by which each nation gains goods, services, or capital it needs but lacks. The growth of commercial relationships, even those of unequal benefit, enriches all parties; the disruption of commerce carries costs for all. The exchange of goods and services fosters national wealth and well-being, the enhancement of which is a principal purpose of the state. At the same time, interdependence breaks down the barriers between nations that the state was created to erect and defend. Reliance on the markets and products of others qualifies each nation's independence and makes its wealth and power hostage to the interruption of commerce. Economic power and vulnerability are thus the two sides of a single door. Dependence on specific items of exchange gauges vulnerability to economic pressure from others. The ability to resist dictation from foreign peoples is among the main purposes for which states are established.

Economic Measures

Relative gain or injury from sudden, state-instigated changes in commercial relations varies between societies, economic sectors, and regions of nations. Those changes that most directly affect national power and well-being are of greatest concern to the state. Shifts in established patterns of commerce generally affect one nation more than another. An abrupt relaxation of restrictions on trade and financial flows may strengthen one national economy in relation to another. A sudden curtailment of such flows may be tolerable to one but unendurable by another.

A state that is better able than others to tolerate such changes can use this advantage to induce or compel them to make decisions favorable to its interests by opening or restricting its markets. Such *economic measures* alter the commercial relationships between nations to secure advantages or send political signals for the states that adopt them.

Used *strategically*, economic measures manipulate trade and finance to regulate the balance of power and relationships between states. They seek to foster cooperative relations with other states and to nurture their wealth and power, or to isolate them and weaken their national strength and potential. Used *tactically*, economic measures apply commerce as a lever to move foreign leaders' minds. They seek to stimulate foreign states to make specific policy changes, to adopt desirable behavior, or to refrain from objectionable behavior.

Strategic Uses of Economic Measures

A state may have a strategic interest in bolstering the independence and enhancing the national strength and potential of another state or group of states. Economic aid in the form of budgetary transfers and subsidies to facilitate policy changes in such states, as well as investment incentives to direct private capital to the development of strategic sectors of their economies, can help to accomplish the strengthening of such states over time. A state may have a further interest in submerging competition in cooperation, broadening and deepening relations, enhancing influence, or gaining access for its commerce in another state or group of states. Lowering barriers to economic interaction realizes such interests. The granting of trade preferences, tariff reductions, or tax benefits stimulates the growth of commercial exchange between societies. Measures to ease the operation and lower the costs of transportation and communication links do the same.

If carried to their logical conclusion, such measures may result in a common market, including the establishment of joint institutions to regulate the economies of the states that constitute it. Under such arrangements, international competition is tempered by interdependence. Conflict among the states party to such arrangements to foster interdependence becomes increasingly difficult for them to conceive or to carry out.

Employed as an element of strategy in war, blockade and other forms of economic pressure can speed the collapse of an enemy's capacity and will to resist. In times of peace, a state may also have a strategic interest in weakening a state that it regards as a potential enemy, in impairing its capabilities, or in constraining its international alternatives. Prudently targeted economic measures can often serve these interests. Such measures include the control of exports with military applications or relevance to strategic economic sectors. They may involve preclusive buying of raw materials or commodities to deny them to the adversary's economy. They can include administrative, tariff, and tax barriers to trade and investment. They may extend to the outright prohibition of trade and financial transactions, the severance of transportation and communication links, the seizure of assets, and the blacklisting of corporations and individuals who circumvent these restrictions.

Such economic measures can retard the growth of national power and potential in the target state. They may gain time for other factors or instruments of statecraft to take effect. A strategy based on aggressive trade and financial controls is, however, risky, difficult to implement, and uncertain of success.

Treated as an enemy or outlaw, the target state may see little reason not to behave as such. If it views the economic measures imposed on it as a credible threat to its survival and freedom of action, it may choose to go to war before its military capabilities begin seriously to erode.

Restrictions on commerce often take years, if not decades, to have much impact. They cannot be effective unless all states in a position to circumvent them respect and enforce them. Concerting such a collective effort is always a difficult, and sometimes an impossible, diplomatic task. Unmet demand in the target nation may in time lead to the emergence of suppliers of the embargoed goods and services in other countries that originally did not produce or trade them, rendering continued enforcement of the embargo increasingly untenable. Ironically, efforts at economic isolation may stimulate growth and employment rather than decline in the target economy, as import substitution and forced policies of autarky foster investment in industries that would otherwise have been uneconomic.

A state's objectives sometimes go beyond the weakening of another's capacity to make war. They may encompass the removal of an objectionable government from power and its replacement by one less hostile. This is achieved most efficiently by conquest. It can, however, sometimes be accomplished by a strategy of political pressure and covert support for resistance and insurrection. Economic strangulation is a useful addition to a strategy based on measures short of war, as to war itself. It cannot, however, replace more direct and forceful measures to affect foreign political structures and decisions. Economic sanctions are not an effective substitute for war and active measures of subversion. They seldom achieve the overthrow of an objectionable regime even when the economy it rules seems highly vulnerable to them. When they do indeed unseat such a regime, sanctions bequeath a dangerous legacy of economic weakness to its successor.

Economic sanctions and the dislocations they cause may, in fact, strengthen rather than weaken the hold on power of a government targeted by them. Popular resentment of foreign pressure boosts the prestige of leaders who resist it. Peoples will more readily blame foreigners for their suffering than they will their own state or its leaders. As trade and investment withdraw, so do foreign influence and its constraints on government policy. Evidence of foreign hostility justifies the tightening of internal security controls. Isolation reinforces the power of regimes over their people. Efforts at economic strangulation are most easily evaded by ruling elites, whose share of relative wealth and power increases even as the less privileged and politically active are impoverished. Political and economic strain may stimulate emigration, including mass migration to neighboring states. Long-term damage may be done to the target nation's social structure, to its economy, and to its prospects for peaceful coexistence with its neighbors. A more congenial successor regime, when it comes to power, must first struggle to survive this unpropitious socioeconomic legacy. Then it must repair it.

Tactical Uses of Economic Measures

A state may resort to economic measures to induce or coerce alterations in the commercial or political behavior of another. Success in this endeavor depends on the selection of measures involving adequate mass—economic activities in which the state or coalition imposing them disposes of a near monopoly. These measures must also be relevant to the behavior to be altered, affect the interests of those with authority to make the pertinent decisions for the foreign state, be difficult for the target state to counter or offset, and be sustainable at tolerable cost.

Economic measures may be intended to induce or reward good behavior, through economic assistance in the form of cash payments, the extension of credit, or other advantages to subsidize or promote prosperity in a foreign state. Subventions are a time-tested tool of statecraft.

Economic measures may also be coercive or punitive in nature, intended to bring pressure to bear to punish or deter misbehavior by a foreign state. Coercive measures may include restrictions on market access through tariff adjustments, the imposition of licensing requirements, bans on the export or import of selected commodities, or the withdrawal of previous favor, such as economic assistance or trade and investment preferences.

The threat of coercive economic measures is preferable to their actual imposition. Threats can help to deter objectionable policy decisions by the state that is being threatened. Ultimatums add to the pressure to compose differences through negotiation. The actual imposition of economic sanctions adds the costs, complications, and rancor of new grievances to existing disputes.

The efficacy of threatened or actual coercive economic measures is greatest when they are directed at altering the commercial behavior of foreign nations. By definition, such measures strike at commercial and financial interests. They can be concerted with other states that share the interests being pursued to deny ready alternatives to the target economy. Such economic measures can (and should) be aimed directly at affecting the particular interests of those who influence or make decisions on the matters at issue. They can be tailored to have less impact on the state or states imposing them than they do on their target. If negotiations are already under way between the parties, the risk of broad retaliation can be contained by accelerated conclusion of these negotiations. The target state will usually be reluctant to extend contention to additional areas of trade and finance, escalating an economic skirmish into a broader "trade war" that will adversely affect the interests of still more of its citizens.

Coercive economic measures are much less effective when directed at noneconomic objectives, such as the punishment of military or political misbehavior. Threats directed at such objectives invite military or political as well as economic reprisal. Once imposed, economic measures can reach political and military interests only indirectly and imprecisely. The leaders of the target state may be indifferent (or actually pleased by damage) to the commercial and financial interests of those directly affected. They may be able to use their authority to benefit both economically and politically from the market distortions introduced by economic measures. Shortages are market opportunities for leaders in a position to profit from them. Deprivation can rally popular indignation behind the national leadership and against the foreign instigators of economic strain.

The greatest difficulty with the tactical use of economic measures is that, once instituted, they are difficult to end. The state sets the framework for commerce. It is, however, mainly carried out by citizens or corporations. Costs or benefits that the state sees as acceptable for the nation as a whole fall unevenly on individuals, groups, regions, or economic sectors. The redirection of markets by state intervention first generates opposition then creates special interests that rely on the market distortions it has established.

Economic sanctions soon cease to be seen as an instrument by which to modify the behavior of their targets; they become an unassailable feature of the domestic political economy. Debate turns to the relative efficiency with which sanctions are being enforced and the efficacy with which they are inflicting economic hardship on the target nation. The effect, or lack of effect, of this hardship on its policies and practices is seldom evaluated. Ironically, therefore, if sanctions are demonstrably failing to produce the desired policy changes in the target nation, this failure comes to justify their indefinite continuation in force rather than the consideration of alternative approaches. The political burden of proof shifts to those who would end the sanctions. They gain a permanence that was seldom intended. What was meant as a tactical measure thus becomes the central element of strategy.

A state that threatens to impose economic measures on others must ultimately be prepared to do so. To have force, a threatened measure must meet the tests of mass, relevance, impact, irresistibility, and sustainability. To be effective as a method of dispute settlement, both threats and steps to implement them need a context, such as a negotiating process, that provides a means by which to reach a mutually agreeable compromise before the threats must be fully carried out. The target of the threatened measures must perceive that it has reasonable alternatives to suffering the consequences of continuing defiance of the demands being levied on it. The tactical use of economic measures is thus, like other coercive tools of statecraft, an adjunct, not an alternative to negotiation.

THE NONVIOLENT USE OF MILITARY POWER

Military capabilities are an essential element of national power. They deter the use of force by other states. They provide a state with the ultimate means to coerce other states into adjustments in relations. The ability to use force causes adversaries to heed efforts to obtain such adjustments by measures short of war, such as diplomatic persuasion.

States develop military capabilities to deter or make war. These capabilities are, however, also uniquely suited to actions short of war by which they can bring their power to bear on others. Such nonviolent military actions include shows of force, the provision of training and logistical support to the armed forces of other states, intervention to restore order, the monitoring of truces or verification of the implementation of agreements, and the delivery of emergency assistance.

Show of Force

The political impact of military prowess depends on adversaries' perceptions of it. It is therefore useful from time to time to call military capabilities to the attention of adversaries. Temporary deployments, military exercises, naval visits, and familiarization tours for foreign militaries do this.

A timely reminder of the capacity to use force (or to block attempts by others to use force) to compel settlement of a dispute strengthens the hand of negotiators. This is especially so when the matters under negotiation touch on vital interests.

The possibility of a resort to force is then most credible. A show of force emphasizes the possibility of escalated and intensified confrontation. It is the use of force to persuade rather than to dictate.

It is often best to stage a show of force at a distance from the party to be impressed. Too direct and overt a menace may evoke nationalist rage against foreign intimidation. This may impair, rather than enhance, the other side's freedom to yield what it must yield to resolve the dispute.

Training and Logistical Support

A state may have a strategic or even vital interest in the balance of power between other states and in the outcome of possible confrontations between them. The capacity to reinforce allies and friends deters attack on them and bolsters their ability to resist it when deterrence fails. The gift or sale of weapons and the conduct of training and joint exercises with the armed forces of allies and friends serve these purposes as well as others. Such military assistance is an important instrument of statecraft.

Military assistance provides tangible evidence of an interest in the security of allies and friends and their ability to defend themselves. It ensures access to their military leaders. It provides a means by which to influence their military decisions and actions.

Commonality of equipment and munitions facilitates resupply of allied and friendly forces in times of crisis or war. The ability to bolster them with immediately usable equipment, parts, and munitions leaves open the option of an indirect, supporting role in combat rather than direct participation in it. Strengthening the military capabilities of allies and friends raises the threshold at which others must join in their defense.

Training and joint exercises demonstrate effective partnership and give deterrent credibility to alliance. Such activities build common doctrine and operating concepts. They are the essential basis for coordinated action and cooperation on the battlefield.

Military aid to insurgents should be given clandestinely or indirectly. Insurgencies fare best when they appear not to be the tools of foreign powers. The provision of training and munitions to insurgent forces is an act of war against the government they seek to overthrow. It invites reprisal from that government. A state providing such assistance must be confident of its ability to deter reprisal against its territory and interests at home and abroad, or be willing to accept the risk of such reprisal.

Overt aid to rebellion invites overt retaliation; covert assistance invites covert reprisal. Governments under serious pressure from insurgents are, however, seldom eager to add escalating conflict with powerful external enemies to their existing difficulties. Lack of clarity about the source, amount, and channels of foreign aid to rebels against such governments may give rulers an excuse to refrain from retaliatory action against those who provide such aid.

Intervention to Restore Order or Provide Relief

A state or society that descends into civil strife or anarchy is a cancer on the international body politic that endangers its neighbors and its region. Segments of its population may destabilize neighboring states by seeking refuge there. Its domestic violence may spill over its borders. Such internal disorder is a threat to international order and the interests of other states. It invokes the logic of reason of system.

The collapse of a state therefore invites foreign intervention. The purpose may be to provide humanitarian relief or to impose order. Direct or indirect intervention by states in the internal proceedings of others is never disinterested. States carry out such intervention as a matter of self-interest, the interest of the international state system, or both. Of these motives, the most compelling is self-interest. Intervention that does not involve clearly articulated national interests is difficult to sustain in the face of setbacks. Few publics are willing for long to support abstract principles at the price of tangible sacrifices of their own blood and treasure.

The military are specialists in the projection of national power. Military prowess in logistics is developed for this purpose. In addition to their capacity to apply force, the military provide a state with a unique capability to respond to natural disaster and human emergency at home and abroad. The armed forces can often deliver food, emergency shelter, and medical supplies; build camps for displaced populations; and establish temporary administrative structures with greater speed and at greater distance than any other instrument of the state. They are usually the most expedient means of accomplishing these tasks both at home and abroad. They are, however, seldom the most efficient means of doing so. Capabilities designed for warfighting are not conceived with financial economy as the primary concern.

The introduction of armed forces—for whatever purpose—into an area where combat is taking place is a show of force, implying the willingness to engage in combat. The pacifying effect of a military presence derives from the expectation that it is both capable of using force and willing to do so, if necessary or provoked. If there is no willingness to use force and to accept the consequences of doing so, the military are not the appropriate instrument of statecraft. Their deployment then invites either humiliation for the nation or coalition that has dispatched them or escalated military intervention to restore lost credibility. If the use of force is ruled out, civilians, despite their lesser capabilities, should be used. If civilians cannot do the job where combat is ruled out, humanitarian intervention probably should not be attempted.

Providing food, medical, and other aid to afflicted populations mitigates the effects of warfare. It makes the carnage and dislocations of violent struggle more tolerable to combatants and noncombatants alike. This tolerance prolongs the fighting and defers the restoration of a tranquil civil society. Whether they use military or civilian agencies to provide humanitarian relief, states must therefore constantly weigh their desire to mitigate the effects of war against their interest in ending it. If the principal interest of those providing relief is the reestablishment of

order, they may wish to act to ensure that one faction contending for power gains quick ascendancy over others, enabling
it to reconstitute the authority of the state. Even a bad government may be preferable to the perpetuation of anarchy or
interminable combat.

Enforcing and Verifying the Implementation of Agreements

Warring states or the parties to a civil war may reach agreement on a truce, exchange of territory, or process by which to
separate, confine, disarm, or amalgamate their armed forces.
They then sometimes ask that foreign forces provide verification
of implementation. Their motives for doing so are usually complex. The parties' request for foreign monitoring may arise naturally from foreign mediation of their dispute. They are likely
to trust third parties more than they trust each other. They may
desire a foreign presence to displace their enemy from strategic locations they were unable to gain in combat. They may
wish to see an immediate enemy withdrawal from territory
they will themselves recover only in stages. One side or the
other may want a "trip wire" to invoke foreign intervention
should combat resume.

The monitoring of truces and cease-fires is more costly than
the verification of territorial exchanges or political agreements.
The end of the fighting under an internationally guaranteed
cease-fire relieves the parties from pressure to conclude a more
permanent settlement of their differences. Thus, the fact that a
cease-fire is monitored effectively may become a potent obsta-
cle to achieving its replacement by a peace. The fighting may
resume if monitoring ceases. The fear that fighting may resume
makes it difficult to withdraw with honor.

Invitations to intervene to enforce agreements between the
parties to civil strife should therefore be greeted with skepticism. An agreement that requires outside intervention for its
enforcement is not truly agreed. It needs enforcement because
the parties expect each other to cheat on their "agreement."

The persistence of their differences will bring the parties into ever greater conflict with those they have mandated to enforce their truce. Unable to fight each other, some among them are likely to turn their guns on the foreign forces in their midst. For these reasons, foreign intervention to assist in ending civil wars may begin without violence but often degenerates into combat. It should be undertaken with this possibility fully in mind.

The introduction of foreign forces to monitor or enforce purely local cease-fires can have the pernicious effect of inhibiting progress toward a general peace. By stabilizing some fronts, foreign soldiers facilitate the concentration of forces on others. By blocking the attacks of the side on the offensive, they allow the side on the defensive to prepare itself for a counteroffensive. They thus become part of the strategic landscape to be used, and abused, by both sides. By forestalling military decision, they produce a war of attrition. In such a war, civilians suffer most. It may be more humane to speed the victory of the faction with the best prospects of rapidly seizing and consolidating power. Often in statecraft, as in life, a decision— even an unpalatable decision—is less harmful than prolonged indecision. When the primary impulse for intervention is the desire to end civilian suffering rather than to decide the specific outcome of the fighting, the earlier the end of the fighting, whoever the victor, the better.

It is therefore wise to agree to monitor truces only when they are comprehensive, or part of a process that will produce a permanent solution between the parties. Even then, a deadline should be set for the withdrawal of military monitors. Such a deadline puts pressure on the parties to make peace. The verification of territorial exchanges or the carrying out of military aspects of agreements between previously warring parties, by welcome contrast, comes automatically to an end when implementation has been completed or has failed.

The skills of observation and reporting that truce monitoring involves are not skills peculiar to the military. Nevertheless, only military monitoring of military violations is credible, and only the military can serve as a convincing "trip wire." Truce monitoring is thus a task the military alone can undertake. It thrusts soldiers, however, into a world of mediation, compromise, and diplomatic uncertainty for which their training in the arts of war ill prepares them. Forces assigned to monitor truces or the implementation of agreements perform an intelligence collection and military-diplomatic task most closely resembling that of military attachés. They must be trained to do quasi-diplomatic work. Their combat skills decline; they require extensive retraining once their tour of duty as monitors is behind them.

Military Deployments for Operations Other than the Use of Force

The essential role and unique expertise of the military is the use of force. Their deployment, whatever its intention, signals willingness to respond to violence in kind. If no such signal is intended, it is better not to deploy the armed forces but to use civilian means to accomplish the mission at hand.

Shows of force are empty and ultimately counterproductive unless backed by the perceived determination to use force if necessary. Similarly, the deployment of the armed forces to a combat zone evokes a different response than the deployment of civilians, both where they are deployed and at home. Soldiers are expected to be able to defend themselves and to defend one another. Local combatants may see the deployment of foreign soldiers rather than civilians in their midst as inviting violent challenge. Attacks on soldiers have a legitimacy that attacks on civilians do not. Military casualties invoke the duty of the armed forces to protect their comrades by counterattack, and lead to demands in their homeland that they be allowed to do so or be withdrawn from danger. The state may come to face an unwelcome choice between military escalation or humiliation.

The withdrawal of armed forces because they are suffering casualties leads to loss of military credibility. Civilian casualties, tragic as they are, do not have this result. Civilians are not expected to be able to defend themselves. They can be withdrawn without any implication of military cowardice or national lack of fortitude.

Sound statecraft therefore dictates caution in the use of military capabilities to do things that can be done by civilians. If the military must be used, statesmen should normally seek the earliest possible replacement of the armed forces by civilian agencies. This action restores to civilian agencies and non-governmental organizations a role that is normally theirs. It saves money. It reduces the risk of military humiliation. It preserves the deterrent value of the armed forces.

The state maintains armed forces to ensure its survival and to advance and defend its national interests by force, when it is necessary. Prudence dictates that, to the extent possible, the nation's military be not long diverted from these tasks, which they alone can perform.

THE USE OF FORCE

Peace is the acceptance of the status quo as preferable to its violent overthrow. The price of peace is the deterrence of challenges to it by military measures short of war. Deterrence rests on perceived readiness to punish those who might break the peace with levels of damage to their military forces or other elements of national power and well-being that would be unacceptable to them. Deterrence requires constant effort to convince opponents not only that the potential costs to them of armed conflict will outweigh probable gains but also that aggression on their part cannot succeed. A weak state will strive to conceal its weakness and seek to induce its opponents to make inflated estimates of its military capabilities. A strong state will wish to advertise its military prowess through open displays of its capabilities and disclosure of its plans to enhance them.

War is the systematic application of organized violence by one state to another to accomplish adjustments in political, economic, cultural, or military relations. In the contention between states, such violent use of force is the ultimate argument of statecraft. War dictates rather than persuades. Armed conflict is expensive in lives and treasure for both victor and vanquished. Its end is not easily foretold and its outcome is seldom sure. Low-intensity and limited conflict are part of a spectrum whose other end is a war of annihilation. That spectrum is all too easily traversed. Violent action by a state against another is therefore justified only when measures short of it cannot suffice and when prospective gains outweigh sacrifices and costs.

The Decision to Go to War

The purpose of war is to secure a more advantageous peace. Its success lies in making future wars improbable. The motive of war is to compel an enemy to agree to or to acquiesce in terms and conditions it would not otherwise accept. If victory does not produce this result, the sacrifices required to produce victory are in vain. War is an instrument of policy; its success is measured by its political results. It is how wars end and what they end in, not how they begin or what happens during them, that gives wars meaning.

For war to end, the vanquished must accept both the military reality and the political consequences of their defeat. Those who would resort to the use of force must therefore consider not just whether they can prevail over the enemy and bear the cost of doing so. They must ask whether and how they can obtain the enemy's surrender or capitulation to the terms they would impose. The enemy must be brought to accept and respect a resolution of the issues that gave rise to war on terms it originally considered inadmissible. If the use of force fails to produce such adjustment in relations between belligerents, it is more likely to complicate and embitter these issues than to advance them toward resolution. Future war will be more, rather than less, probable.

A humbled adversary must be brought to regard the concessions defeat imposes as final, and not subject to later revision or reversal. It must put the hatred born of strife sufficiently behind it to live in peace with those who have just humiliated it on the battlefield. These results do not come easily. A war may be won by shaping the attitudes and actions of the enemy. A peace is won by shaping the attitudes and actions of the defeated. The need to produce such a postwar condition of peace must guide the formulation of war aims, the conduct of the war, and the diplomacy of its termination.

War Aims

War aims are the declared and undeclared objectives for which a war is fought. Whether declared or undeclared, war aims must be attainable at an acceptable level of national mobilization, casualties, and expense. Otherwise, they are a recipe for protracted and indecisive conflict or for constantly escalating political, economic, and military demands on the belligerents. War aims that touch the supreme or vital interests of the enemy will invoke a corresponding level of effort by the enemy. The enemy's escalation will then call for proportionally greater sacrifice from those proclaiming and pursuing such aims. Unrealistic objectives often end by demanding previously unthinkable, escalating levels of effort for their attainment.

War aims that are declared must be designed to be quickly attainable. Once the objectives they embody have been attained, a hard-pressed foe must see acquiescence in what it has lost as preferable to continued fighting. If the terms for relief from further attack are too harsh, they will stiffen and prolong enemy resistance rather than hasten capitulation. War aims should therefore be as moderate as national interest allows. The clamor to expand them in the enthusiasm born of military success should be greeted with skepticism. An expansion of war aims can galvanize an enemy to a higher level of effort by appearing to pose a more far-reaching and fundamental threat to its interests. It can also alarm other states interested in the outcome of the conflict, possibly stimulating them to step up their assistance to the enemy or to join in the fighting themselves.

Undeclared war aims should be implicit in victory and self-executing, requiring no acceptance by the defeated enemy for their realization. Attempts to impose additional terms on an enemy after combat has ended are difficult. The victor's ability to extract further concessions from the enemy is greatly weakened by the suspension of combat. The public expectation is then that the fighting is or should be over. Few will wish to renew the sacrifices inherent in war. Most will look to an early peace to consolidate military victory. No government will wish to have to explain why its apparent victory was deceptive or incomplete. The threat to resume the offensive therefore steadily loses credibility once battle has halted.

The Conduct of War

The achievement of the policy objectives for which a war was fought, not damage done to the enemy, defines success in war. The incorporation of these objectives into a durable peace consolidates war's success. Peace requires the revision of relationships with former adversaries. The enlistment of erstwhile enemies in a stable postwar balance of power buttresses peace. War is properly conducted to shape the peace to follow it. But war quickly develops its own political dynamic. Strategic vision and the requirement to shape the peace are all too easily set aside by governments excited by warfare.

The natural instincts of an aroused and vengeful populace in wartime demand destruction of all that the enemy holds dear. Such passion should not prevail over considered judgments about where and how force can be applied most effectively to bring the enemy to terms. Weapons are tools to change men's minds and thereby shape a more secure future. They should be employed to accomplish this end with all the precision that intelligence and technology will permit. Used with purposive economy, force can often cripple the enemy military, compel its leadership to seek an end to the fighting, or catalyze favorable change in its leadership.

The targets of military action should be carefully selected for both their military and political effect. The primary focus must be the maiming of the enemy's military, the reduction of its capacity and will to resist, and the shaping of its decision to capitulate. Devastation of targets unrelated to the enemy's warfighting capacity seldom stimulates it to question its ability to prevail on the battlefield. If the enemy's war aims have popular support, such damage is more likely to rally its people behind resistance than to divide them from their leadership. It therefore seldom produces a judgment by the enemy that it must accept the terms it has been offered. Damage to the enemy's infrastructure beyond that required to compel its capitulation is also risky. It may leave a defeated enemy so vulnerable as to tempt aggression against it by others formerly deterred from attacking it.

If it is a mistake to adopt immoderate war aims or to strike indiscriminately, it is equally a mistake to soften those blows that are delivered. Force applied halfheartedly or with less than devastating effect emboldens an enemy to continue its resistance. If the effect on the targets of military action is less than overwhelming, the enemy will discount the additional damage it might suffer from continued resistance. Self-restraint in the application of force therefore commonly generates a pattern of continuing escalation in warfare. The enemy becomes more and more able to bear what it once would have felt to be intolerable. This prolongs war.

Half measures also leave unbowed and vengeful enemies. Some among an enemy population will always deny the reality of their defeat and reject the legitimacy of the terms by which the war was ended. War must be conducted to reduce the numbers of such doubters. Defeat is most easily tolerated by those who know that, even with greater effort, they could not have prevailed. Even if little or no territorial gain is sought, the seizure of significant territory may therefore be necessary to bring the enemy to terms. The lines of control when the fighting stops shape the contours of the peace. Diplomats must bargain on the basis of what warriors have seized or lost. Territory, even more than war booty and prisoners, is something to trade for an enemy's acceptance of the adjustments necessary for peace.

The use of force should therefore be limited in its political, economic, and military objectives, but unlimited in the ferocity with which it strikes its targets. Brutally precise military action against an enemy can hasten its acceptance of terms, reduce the challenge of its postwar reconstruction and reconciliation, and speed profit from economic and other cooperation with it. The enemy must not doubt that further resistance will produce further humiliation. This realization shortens wars, lessens civilian and military casualties on both sides, and promotes reconciliation to defeat. It can preserve the enemy's capacity, though weakened by defeat, to resume constructive participation in international affairs.

The need to end a war at the right moment dictates that there be continuing contact with an enemy as combat proceeds. Military science recognizes the need to maintain constant contact with enemy forces to avoid surprise and preserve options for attack. In diplomacy, too, contact with an enemy must never be lost. Otherwise, statecraft is blinded and its tongue is tied. Politics or concerns about diplomatic security often compel the withdrawal of representation from an enemy capital in wartime. This is disadvantageous. If diplomatic relations must be broken, alternative but less obvious channels of communication must replace them. Such contact is essential to preclude miscalculation by either side and to enable the negotiation of an end to the fighting when that is appropriate.

War Termination

Victory marks success in combat; the translation of victory into a peace that can last defines success in war. For a war to end, the enemy must either agree to negotiated terms or surrender unconditionally. In either case, the basic terms of the peace should be agreed to before victory is declared, military operations or occupations are halted, and peace is proclaimed. The bargaining power of the victor ebbs as fighting ends and memory of battle recedes. Explicit acceptance by the defeated enemy of the terms of capitulation is essential. Such acceptance implicates the enemy leadership in these terms, endorses the peace, and legitimizes defeat and complicates efforts to reverse it.

An inconclusive peace is as bad as an inconclusive war, and fraught with greater uncertainty. Diplomacy therefore does not cease during wartime; it becomes focused on the shaping of tomorrow's peace with today's enemy. Soldiers fight wars to produce a clear military decision. Diplomats must ensure that war produces a clear political result. That result depends on the lines of control when the fighting stops but is defined in diplomatic interaction between the parties to the conflict.

Any negotiation is the rearrangement of a relationship between the parties. No more fundamental rearrangement of relationships exists than that produced by the ending of a war and the conclusion of a peace. The terms by which wars end create the boundaries of a new world for victor and vanquished alike. It is easier for the victor to accept the changed situation than for the vanquished. War subdues peoples but does not capture their hearts. A peace based on humiliation of the vanquished contains the germs of renewed warfare. Diplomacy must reconcile the vanquished to their defeat and convince them of the benefits of the peace.

Consolidating the Peace

Peace is a pattern of stability acceptable to those with the capacity to disturb it by violence. The speed and manner in which the terms of peace are implemented have much to do with the degree to which peace can be consolidated.

The transition to peace may involve occupation of all or part of the enemy's territory. Occupation, no matter how benevolent, is ultimately a corrupting experience for the occupiers and a traumatic one for those occupied. The skills of occupation are those characteristic of police, administrators, and politicians, not of the military. Occupation duty corrodes armies. They lose their warfighting skills, develop a garrison mentality, and are brutalized, deprofessionalized, and politicized by their internal security duties. The consolidation of peace rests on acceptance by the defeated of the legitimacy of the postwar order. Civilian populations do not regard military rule, especially rule by foreign soldiers, as legitimate.

Occupations should therefore be as brief as possible. If they must be prolonged, the occupying power should seek the earliest possible transfer of authority to civilian police and the administrative cadre to remove the military from internal security duties. This transfer restores the military to its accustomed role and gives less time for serious friction with the defeated populace to emerge. It leaves open the possibility that frustration and resentment will not erase initial good impressions of a disciplined and well-behaved occupation force. Such good impressions of a victor's military reinforce the willingness of a defeated enemy to embrace postwar rapprochement.

When war ends without occupation, the consolidation of the peace is a no less subtle task. It depends on mutual confidence and respect between victor and vanquished. This requires scrupulous adherence by both to the terms by which combat has ended. It also levies special demands of humility and self-restraint on the victor. Nothing is gained by contemptuous treatment of a defeated enemy or disparagement of its resourcefulness in war. This adds insult to defeat, even as it devalues the statecraft, generalship, and sacrifices that were required for victory. Magnanimity toward a defeated foe and praise for its valor in battle help to reconcile it both to its newly reduced status and to its revised relationship with its victors.

Establishment of relations of mutual respect and cooperation between victor and vanquished is the basis of peace between them. The restoration of peace gives war its meaning. The reduction of mutual animosity and the rediscovery of common interests gives peace permanence. The art of crafting peace demands no less of the victor than the achievement of victory in war.

DIPLOMATIC MANEUVER

DIPLOMATIC STRATEGY AND TACTICS

The way of the state, like all paths in human affairs, is subject to the actions of others and to accidents of fortune. The essence of strategy is the effort to gain and retain the initiative, and to minimize the effects of chance. Strategy unites foresight and determination. It combines capabilities with opportunities to achieve broad, predetermined ends through skillful maneuver that minimizes costs.

Strategy is concerned with long-term advance. It must be applied through tactics. Tactics are the detailed plans and means by which strategy advances in the short term. Tactical actions pursue gains or defend interests in particular circumstances. The sum of tactical gains may constitute strategic advance, but the results of disparate tactics uninspired by a strategic design do not add up to a strategy. To allow tactics to define or drive strategy is opportunism. This risks the achievement of short-term gain at the expense of longer-term overextension, exhaustion, and vulnerability to reversal.

Grand Strategy

Grand strategy unites military and diplomatic strategy. It integrates all elements of national power in policies calculated to advance or defend national interests and concerns in light of anticipated trends and events. Grand strategy is directed at the achievement of the greatest gain at the least military, political, economic, and cultural cost to the state and the nation. It commonly aims at the achievement of a state's objectives without the uncertainties and expense of war. Grand strategy prepares, however, for the contingency of war. It seeks to ensure conditions that will produce victory when war occurs.

Grand strategy may contemplate the revolutionary overthrow of the existing international system and the reordering of relations between states. Such a strategy may have a diplomatic component but is ultimately military in nature. Revolutions involve a level of violent ruthlessness that diplomacy does not comprehend. Diplomacy is the adjustment of relations between states by mutual agreement. More commonly, grand strategy seeks to use the existing international order to the benefit of the state. Accomplishing this is the central task of diplomatic strategy.

Diplomatic Strategy

Diplomatic strategy seeks advantage for the state by measures short of war. It is directed at ensuring that as many paths as possible lead to peaceful gains vis-à-vis other states and as few as possible lead to setbacks, the requirement to resort to force, or the need to defend against aggression. Diplomatic strategy must be judged by what it prevents as much as by what it achieves.

Diplomatic strategy gains leverage for national capabilities by positioning the state to apply them at an auspicious time. Such diplomatic maneuver can increase the mass, relevance, impact, irresistibility, and sustainability of a state's capabilities in relation to other states. Diplomatic strategy and tactics decide the moment when these capabilities can be most efficaciously applied to other states.

In wartime, diplomatic strategy supports military strategy through the management of relations with allies and the disruption of enemy alliances. It strives to translate battlefield victories into postwar gains in the security, well-being, and international influence of the state. It struggles to minimize the consequences of military setbacks or defeat.

Diplomatic strategy, like grand strategy, is ultimately the responsibility of statesmen rather than diplomats. The primary task of diplomats is the tactical implementation of strategy where they are assigned, rather than its formulation. Diplomats are nevertheless active participants in the formulation of diplomatic strategy. No strategy can succeed unless it is tactically implementable. Plans are of little value unless those who must implement them understand them and are committed to them. Nor can those who plan implement their designs directly or adjust them to each circumstance their strategy may confront. Statesmen must check strategy against tactical realities. They must ensure that those who are to achieve their strategic objectives understand these objectives and consider the statesmen's concept for reaching them practical and feasible.

Varieties of Diplomatic Strategy

Diplomatic strategies may be passively defensive, actively defensive, or assertive.

Diplomatic strategy may be directed at the consolidation and gradual improvement of an advantageous status quo. Such a defensive diplomatic strategy foresees no immediate challenge that could be fatal to the existing international order. It assumes that the pattern of relations between major states will be relatively constant. It foresees that international change will be gradual or confined, rather than abrupt or systemic. In such circumstances, strategy may take the form of a broad set of essentially unchanging guidelines for tactical response to challenges and opportunities that arise. Such a defensive approach levies few strategic demands on statecraft once a basic set of strategic guidelines has been created.

The risk in such a defensively reactive diplomatic strategy is national complacency and passivity. The consequent failure to act to prevent or mitigate trends may, in time, permit unfavorable changes in the international strategic environment. A strategy of active defense anticipates trends and attempts either to redirect them or to turn them to advantage. It searches for tactical openings by which to improve the position of the state in relation to others.

No international order is everlasting. No state is eternally strong or forever weak. No alliance or enmity is perpetual. The decline of strong states, the rise of weak ones, or the rearrangement of relations between former allies and enemies can throw the international order into kaleidoscopic change, fundamentally altering the environment in which both grand and diplomatic strategy must operate. This poses a challenge for states privileged by the order that is passing, and an opportunity for those who were disadvantaged by it.

When the international order is in flux, the past and present are no longer a clear guide to the future. Continuation of a defensive diplomatic strategy based on tactical response to events then places strategic interests at risk. In circumstances in which the international order is increasingly undefined or is redefining itself unfavorably, states formerly devoted to the defense and preservation of the status quo must become assertively demanding. They must redefine the strategic environment to their advantage, or see others redefine it to their own benefit. The transition to such an assertive diplomatic strategy is often difficult for a state that had prospered in the now collapsing status quo.

Transition tests the wisdom of governments. Form will sooner or later arise from chaos, but it needs help to do so rapidly and auspiciously. Those present at the creation of a new order have a unique opportunity to shape it to the advantage of their state's national interests and concerns. Speed in seizing this opportunity makes every difference. The initial contours of a new international order tend to outlast the forces that sculpted them. A state not blessed with the wherewithal to establish a universal or feudal order centered on itself must be concerned, above all, with the nature of the emerging international state system and the norms that system entails. These will determine the potential for both diplomatic maneuver and peaceful change once the new order consolidates itself.

An assertive diplomatic strategy actively seeks broad change in the existing international order. It considers rapprochement with former adversaries while reevaluating inherited alliances and partnerships. Such a diplomatic strategy courts rising powers. It attempts to neutralize the hostility of potential adversaries. If it cannot do this, it seeks to balance or contain them. An alertly assertive diplomatic strategy reexamines its pattern of participation in existing international organizations and regulatory regimes, and strives to adjust these institutions and their activities to its greater benefit. If it cannot do so, it considers the possibility of replacing them.

A wise state yields gracefully to what it cannot resist, while attempting to wrest every advantage from unavoidable adjustments to emerging realities. Such a state contrives the timing and manner of its concessions to other states. It thus gains benefits for giving up earlier what it would have had to give up later without compensation. A state that practices assertive diplomacy reforges the instruments of its statecraft to meet the new challenges before it. It seeks to create opportunities through diplomatic maneuver rather than waiting passively for them to arise from changing circumstances. It strives to lead rather than to follow others into a new era.

DIPLOMATIC MANEUVER

Diplomatic maneuver is the process by which states reposition themselves vis-à-vis other states. They do so to gain strategic advantage in political, economic, or military matters or to forestall developments damaging to their strategic position. There are thirteen basic maneuvers to accomplish this. Each may be carried out by purchase, a negotiated exchange of benefits, or coercion. None may be carried out by unilateral action; each requires actions by two or more states to succeed.

These diplomatic maneuvers are (1) the exaction of concessions from other states; (2) the accommodation or appeasement of other states' demands; (3) the containment and ostracism of adversaries to hamper their achievement of their national objectives; (4) the management of tensions with adversaries through détente; (5) constructive engagement with adversaries to alter their behavior and expand cooperation with them; (6) rapprochement with adversaries and enemies; (7) estrangement from former partners and allies in order to make partners and allies of their adversaries and enemies; (8) the formation and dissolution of ententes, coalitions, and alliances; (9) the achievement and maintenance of a position of monopoly control; (10) the domination of a state or region to the exclusion of others' influence; (11) agreements to practice mutual restraint in the pursuit of unilateral advantage in capabilities; (12) agreements to share power and its benefits; and (13) the use of international regulatory regimes and organizations.

Exaction, Accommodation, and Appeasement

If a state covets and wishes to obtain something controlled by another state, it must persuade or compel the other state to concede what it wants or continue to do without it. It may seek territory, an ethnic minority and its land, the use of bases and facilities, an outlet to the sea, transit rights, natural resources, commodities, markets, technology, or wealth. A state should not demand what it will be unable either to take or to pay for with something of equal value to the state from which it is demanding it. To do so is to court futility and a reputation for fecklessness.

A state may have many motives for desiring concessions from another beyond simply obtaining the item at issue. It may desire to weaken the other state by depriving it of that item, or to preempt still another state's efforts to gain strategic advantage by acquiring or using the item. It may wish to punish another state, to obtain reparations for injuries suffered at its hands, or to compel it to show deference. A state may aspire to a privileged position as the protector of a minority population of compatriots or coreligionists in another state. It may seek to annex the lands of such a minority or to establish them as a friendly buffer state. It may want to extinguish the independence of another state and to annex its entire territory and population.

Confronted by demands of any kind from another state, a state must consider both the long- and short-term consequences of acceding to such *exactions*. It must weigh the balances of perceived power and fervor between it and the other state with regard to the issues in contention in order to judge whether it can gain most by bargaining or by refusing to do so. If a state decides to negotiate, it must consider what it will require in exchange for meeting the other state's demands. A state seeking to negotiate with another must decide whether it will seek to link still other issues to those originally in contention in an effort to compose a fairer bargain. Such a state should consider whether support from others might strengthen its position and what price it would have to pay in terms of its other interests to entice others to provide such support. Are there unilateral actions it can take to counter the demands of the other state or to render them moot? Can gaining time enable it to improve its position? Is the matter one on which it will eventually have to yield? If so, can it obtain something in return for an *accommodation* of the other state now that it could not gain if forced to yield to it later?

A state seeking only limited adjustment of the status quo may be appeased by meeting enough of its demands to reduce the sources of tension with it and to curb further ambition on its part for disadvantageous change. Attempted *appeasement* of a state seeking to overthrow or make major alterations in the status quo is, however, more likely to stimulate its appetite for further concessions than to sate it. Before responding to demands from another state, especially one more powerful, a state must therefore assess the other's overall strategy and objectives, as well as the basis for the other's claim. Failure to address the limited demands of a bitterly aggrieved and powerful foreign state can be as dangerous as naively granting concessions to a power with larger ambitions.

Containment, Détente, and Constructive Engagement

A state may seek to dominate other states or to extend its borders and spheres of influence in ways that threaten the vital or strategic interests of other states. It may seek to change the existing international order step-by-step or to do so in a revolutionary manner that is contemptuous of international norms. Whatever their differences on other matters may be, states that benefit from the status quo will share an interest in combining to check the ambitions of another state to overthrow the status quo. This interest can form the basis of a coalition effort to deny an expansionist or revolutionary power opportunities to expand its presence or influence abroad and to counter its efforts to do so. Such *containment* aims at restricting the access of the state that is its target to the benefits of normal international relationships, at weakening it, and at retarding its efforts to strengthen itself. Containment seeks to erode the potential aggressor's ambition, dull its revolutionary fervor, or change its political complexion through protracted frustration of its goals.

States that are locked in a broadly adversarial relationship may wish to reduce the danger of conflict by diminishing the level of tension between them. *Détente* is a diplomatic maneuver that accepts the existence of fundamental conflicts of national interests and concerns with an adversary state and seeks to manage rather than to eliminate these conflicts. It rests on the effort to identify common interests that can be used to add stabilizing elements of cooperation to a relationship that, it assumes, will remain essentially antagonistic. The purpose of détente is to give a potential enemy state disincentives to unilateral action, to soften its hostility, and to gain a measure of influence over its decision making. Détente promotes dialogue that can lessen the danger of miscalculation or inadvertent provocation by either side. It does not signal an end to rivalry.

Rivalry can continue even when the state that is the object of détente is a revolutionary power whose ardor for radical change has begun to ebb. In that case, détente can promote the gradual incorporation of such a state into the existing international order by giving it an increasing stake in the stable continuation of that order. By giving such a state practical reasons to cooperate, and by broadening interaction with its government and people, détente can also serve to some extent as an instrument for the subversion of dogmatism. As long as fundamental conflicts of interest with it persist, however, the relationship with such a state will remain basically adversarial.

Conversely, when an adversarial relationship with another state is primarily based on differences in ideology or on a few relatively narrow conflicts of interest, it may be possible to establish a relationship with it in which elements of cooperation gradually come greatly to outweigh elements of competition. Such *constructive engagement* allows common interests to be pursued with another state, even as sharp differences continue to exist with it on some issues. The central element of constructive engagement is the conduct of diplomatic dialogue on matters of common strategic concern. This dialogue aims at expanding areas of agreement and cooperation between two formerly estranged states, even as both acknowledge that they have apparently irreconcilable differences on some specific issues. Setting aside such differences allows both sides to work to narrow them. Deferring final resolution of disputes enables experience with the successful pursuit of common interests to create a better context for resolving such disputes.

In its most developed form, constructive engagement may be comprehensive, attempting to connect bureaucracies, institutions, and individuals in both states in a myriad of discrete cooperative programs. The entanglement of a broad range of special interests in common endeavors reduces the vulnerability of the emerging relationship to short-term reversal caused by changes of leadership, political flare-ups, or setbacks on either side. It builds domestic support for the new relationship by spreading awareness of its benefits on both sides. Such engagement is inherently subversive of formerly isolated states. It introduces new ideas and awareness of alternatives to established ways broadly throughout their society. This can sow the seeds of political change.

Rapprochement and Estrangement

Shifting balances of power and perception or the emergence of new issues between states will cause an alert state to reexamine and readjust its existing pattern of foreign relations. Such change may make it beneficial for a state to forge a closer relationship with a former rival. *Rapprochement* is a process. It begins when states previously hostile to each other express a desire to search for areas of strategic agreement and to resolve conflicts between them. Rapprochement may be intended to build the basis for entente, or merely to add a deterrent element of uncertainty to the strategic calculations of adversaries and potential enemies. Whatever its motive, rapprochement is a necessary first step to either entente or constructive engagement.

It often happens that a state cannot simultaneously enjoy close relations with two other states between which there is rivalry or enmity. At times, a state may accomplish rapprochement with an adversary only by taking action to demonstrate that it has repudiated a previously cordial relationship or alliance with another state at odds with that adversary. Such deliberate *estrangement* from former friends invites charges of perfidy, but a state's bargaining power is usually enhanced, rather than impaired, by demonstrating its freedom of diplomatic maneuver in pursuit of national interests.

Entente, Coalition, and Alliance

Coalitions add the power of other states to one's own. They can be formed ad hoc, as events occur. A prudent state may, however, wish to prearrange coalitions to deter adverse contingencies or to deal with them if they nonetheless arise. Such *entente* with other states can ease the management of parallel actions or the coming into being of coalitions to meet actual challenges to common interests.

If a challenge can be met only through protracted struggle and is likely to engender continuing clashes between the contending sides, a state may wish to add evidence of resolve and sustained commitment to a *coalition* by formalizing it as an *alliance*. If the challenge is more limited, a state is seldom wise to compromise its freedom of diplomatic maneuver by concluding an alliance. Outmoded alliances are an embarrassing encumbrance on statecraft. It is usually best to ensure that an alliance will expire when the conditions that brought it into being have ended or after an agreed term, unless renewed.

Monopoly and Exclusionary Control

A state may possess a valuable natural resource, commodity, or technology that is either unique or limited in availability. Such a state can bolster its power by rationing the release to others of the things with respect to which it enjoys a *monopoly* or market control. It may do so either on its own or, more commonly, through a coalition or alliance, such as a *cartel*. Exactions that are excessive will, however, breed competition and stimulate the development of substitutes for the products being controlled. Moderation in the exercise of privilege is the key to retaining it.

A state that sits amidst others weaker than it is may be able to incorporate them into a sphere of influence within which it enjoys political, cultural, economic, or military supremacy, while hampering or excluding competition from states outside its sphere. A *sphere of influence* is usually thought of as military in nature, but *exclusionary control* may express itself as a political claque, as a zone of cultural dominance, as a region of privileged and protected markets, or as a monetary zone. The less direct and obvious a state's control of its sphere of influence is, the more durable that control will be. Abuse of supremacy engenders rebellion. Self-restraint and subtlety in the exercise of power avoid costly challenges to dominance.

Mutual Restraint and Power Sharing

Adversaries may mutually wish to restrict the means and places in which they act out their antagonism in order to add stability and predictability to their relationship, to avoid ruinously escalating their competition, or to limit the damage to both should their contention erupt into open struggle. Such agreements to *mutual restraint* seek to constrain military, political, or economic rivalry and to moderate its effects.

Reciprocal measures to ensure against surprise attack, to limit deployments, to reduce armaments, or to decrease the size or limit the structure of armed forces can temper the likelihood that differences between states will lead to war. They can diminish the scope and violence of any conflict that nevertheless ensues. Such measures of *arms control* are defense by diplomatic maneuver rather than military might. So, too, are agreements that establish demilitarized zones and buffer states or guarantee the neutrality of third states. Arms control is an aspect of détente rather than rapprochement. It presupposes continuing antagonism while seeking to modulate mutual hostility. Arms control arrangements can reduce the burden of military defense. They are never a substitute for military vigilance and preparedness.

States may similarly find it in their interest to agree, tacitly or explicitly, to limit their political and economic competition to pursue shared advantage through *power sharing*. They may, for example, undertake to respect each other's political spheres of influence or to coordinate or even jointly exercise political influence in a third state or region. Such arrangements are, however, both difficult to verify and subject to challenge by trends and events in the states and regions where they apply. They are seldom stable. Arrangements to divide or share markets and access to resources are quantifiable and easily policed. Agreements for economic power sharing or mutual restraint of economic competition therefore tend to be more reliable than those related to politics.

Multilateral Arrangements

States may come to share an interest in adopting or codifying common standards for the conduct of international transactions, in raising or lowering barriers to interaction across frontiers, or in promoting or banning specific kinds of behavior by individuals or states. They may also perceive an interest in facilitating political, cultural, economic, or military cooperation among themselves on specified matters. *Multilateral arrangements* are the most efficient way to realize such interests. They find expression in conventions administered by the states party to them, in periodic conferences to consider developments of mutual concern, in collectively managed organizations with administrative or regulatory powers, or in the combination of some or all of these.

States participate in such multilateral arrangements out of a desire to share the burdens and risks of pursuing interests they share with others, to gain prestige, to preempt the influence of rival states, or to broaden international support for their views on matters of concern to them. Such arrangements seek to subject international competition to agreed rules rather than to contests of power between states. Like all experiments in the rule of law, they therefore benefit the weak more than the strong.

DIPLOMATIC NEGOTIATION

The state sets the context and rules for bargaining between institutions and individuals within its domestic jurisdiction. Diplomatic negotiation is bargaining between states. It sets the context and rules for international bargaining between nongovernmental institutions and individuals.

The citizens and corporate entities of a nation are bound by the laws passed by its legislature, the decisions of its courts, and the policies of its executive organs. They negotiate within the context of the social contract these represent. Their agreements are set out in terms standardized by domestic law, legal precedent, and a common understanding of commercial practice. Their commitments will be interpreted or enforced by their domestic legal process. Their failure to live up to these commitments will subject them to legal penalties. They are not at liberty to engage in blackmail or violent reprisal to resolve their differences or gain advantage over one another.

Individuals and businesses that negotiate internationally are subject both to the laws of the state in which they conduct their activities and to the law merchant of international trade. Their contracts are subject to review by the courts or to arbitration.

By contrast, diplomatic negotiation strives to bridge differences between the competing sovereignties of independent states. Sovereign states legislate, make judicial decisions, and execute policies for themselves. They are subject to no overarching authority, laws, or rules other than those they choose for their own reasons mutually to contrive or respect. Often they choose to resolve their differences through dialogue and negotiation. Occasionally, they may decide to refer their controversies to a regulatory or arbitral process on which they have agreed. At other times, they will elect to resolve conflicting interests by resort to coercion, including the organized, purposive violence that is war.

The Purposes of Diplomatic Negotiation

The purpose of diplomatic negotiation is to obtain the acquiescence of another state (or states) in adjustments in relations that advance national interests and address national concerns. A refusal to negotiate is also a form of negotiation. It may prolong a relatively favorable status quo and delay concessions that will ultimately have to be made. It may permit the problem to be resolved by the evolution of other forces. It may induce the other side to improve its offer. It may buy time to create facts or otherwise strengthen or consolidate a position of advantage. Delay may allow a favorable shift in the balance of perceived power between the parties to emerge. It may gain an interval in which to make a show of resolve, gain allies, or prepare for war.

An offer to negotiate need not imply willingness—still less eagerness—to settle the matter in dispute. It may gain time or divert the attention of the other party while efforts are made to strengthen national power and lay a basis for prolonged defiance. It may serve to silence a government's critics while building domestic and international political support for its bargaining position. It may give the politically useful appearance of doing something about a problem without actually having to address it.

When the other party sees much to lose and little to gain in reaching agreement on the issue in dispute, it may be necessary to broaden the controversy or to create additional controversies that can be related to it. The purpose of doing this is to make the status quo no longer acceptable to the other party. Linking new points of difference to resolution of the original dispute can alter the other party's calculus of the costs and benefits of continued intransigence. This can give the other party a reason to compromise it had previously lacked, especially when the issues now linked to the original dispute touch on important interests. Such *linkage* can impel the other party to a negotiation to consider the merits of a package deal. Linkage may take the form of threats or actions to damage the other party's interests, or offers to advance them, or both.

The principal objective of a negotiation may be to overcome serious political differences that have precluded strategic cooperation between states rather than to resolve the issues in apparent dispute between them. When this is the objective, states may choose to resort to creative ambiguity or to a tacit or explicit agreement to disagree. The prerequisite for such deferral of contentious issues is recognition by both sides of common interests of greater importance than the disputes that divide them. The danger in such an approach is that delay may complicate rather than simplify the disputes that have been deferred. Time may thus exacerbate rather than soothe the underlying political differences between the parties. If the factors driving them to cooperate become less important, their original divisions may resurface with added force. Problems that have been successfully deferred for later resolution should therefore not be regarded as settled. Nor should they be left unattended. It may later become necessary actually to resolve them.

Strategy and Tactics

Every international negotiation is directed both at addressing the issues on the table and at redefining the relationships between states. The means by which issues are resolved is a tactical question; the impact those means have on the overall relationship between the parties is a strategic question. The character of international relationships is determined, in no small measure, by the manner in which the states party to them resolve disputes.

Agreements that are fair and that correspond to the interests of the parties to them reconcile them to each other and lay the basis for further cooperation between them. Agreements that are unfair, one-sided, or contrary to the long-term interests of one or more parties to them, breed resentment and sow the seeds of future dissension and conflict. Little is gained, and much may be lost, by the achievement of agreement, even a mutually advantageous agreement, through tactics that are seen by one side as either high- or underhanded. Such tactics leave memories that complicate the resolution of future disagreements with those who believe they have been subjected to sharp practices. Negotiating tactics should always be guided and constrained by strategic objectives. Usually, this dictates that negotiators avoid trickery, deception, or condescension.

The need for straight dealing is never more compelling than in negotiations between strong and weak states. The strong have no need to use underhanded tactics to achieve agreements their power can produce without such tactics. They have every reason to evince respect for the weaker party. Power should speak for itself; strength that is flaunted arouses unnecessary resentment. It is often strategically wise for the strong to refrain from imposing an agreement they have the tactical capacity to impose on a weaker party. Insistence on too much, too soon, may preclude opportunities to gain more, at lesser cost, later.

Negotiated Agreements and Their Alternatives

Agreements are worthless unless they can be and are implemented, if only for long enough to mitigate the underlying disputes from which they arose. Negotiations do not end when agreement is reached; they end when implementation of the agreements they produce is achieved. Negotiations should be conducted, and agreements must be crafted, with a view to the fact that the implementation of an agreement is often the most contentious phase of negotiation.

Agreements, and the relationships they create, persist only as long as the parties who made them consider their continuation in force more advantageous than their abrogation. This is true for agreements between the citizens of a state as well as for agreements between states. Unlike contracts under domestic law, however, there is seldom any court other than that of continuing common interest to which a state can appeal for enforcement of commitments or to penalize other states for refusing to implement them. A state must learn to live with disagreement, negotiate a new accommodation with the other party, persuade it to submit to arbitration, act to compel it to carry out its agreements, or punish it for failing to do so.

International disputes involving a state's vital interests are far more likely to be resolved on the equivalent of the dueling grounds than in the courts of law. A state may submit matters of lesser interest to arbitration if it is too weak to insist on its viewpoint on its own. It is better to lose a relatively minor issue in a tribunal than to lose it on the battlefield. No state, however weak, will easily submit its vital interests to decision by a third party unless it is confident that the decision will favor it.

The absence of compelling external pressure on the governments of sovereign states to adhere to agreements means that they must constantly evaluate the utility of doing so. This judgment springs mainly from their estimate of the severity of probable retaliation from the other party. It must, however, include consideration of the impact of their unilateral repudiation of agreements on other states' willingness to trust them to keep future agreements. Governments may wish to cultivate an international reputation for principled predictability. They may, however, see a reputation for unprincipled pursuit of overriding national interest as in some respects enhancing their power.

For all these reasons, the inability of diplomatic negotiation to produce accord usually leaves disputes to be resolved, if at all, by unilateral maneuver of the parties, including their resort to coercive measures and the use of force. Wars end in negotiations or they continue, if not overtly then by other means or at other times. Negotiations about war termination are a war of the diplomats after the war of the soldiers.

The Context of Diplomatic Negotiation

Diplomatic negotiation crosses frontiers to adjust the relations and harmonize the interests of states and peoples. The perspectives of states and peoples are formed by distinct national histories, languages, and cultures. Their governments are likely to have different views of what is just and proper, how disputes should be managed, how negotiations should be conducted, and how agreement or the lack of it should be expressed.

If the bonds between states and peoples are close, these differences can be relatively easily surmounted. The wider the cultural separation between them and the less their experience of successful interaction with each other, however, the harder it is to ensure common understanding of what is being negotiated. It falls to diplomats to build a common vocabulary and to translate disparate perspectives into shared expectations. This is what is needed for negotiations between states to reach implementable and therefore durable agreements.

Diplomats must prepare themselves to practice the craft of negotiation and the arts of persuasion in places, in a foreign language, and on persons and peoples whose moral and political outlook is always different from, and often at odds with, their own. Their skill and the power and agility of the states they represent, rather than the imposition of principle and precedent, decide the outcome. The alternative to a negotiated settlement of differences is the continuation of the controversy or its resolution in a test of wills and force, not its reference to higher authority.

Diplomats negotiate within an ethical framework established not in codes of law but by the transnational standards of their profession, as informed by the expectations of the international system within which they practice it and the traditions of the states they represent. The professional ethic of diplomacy constitutes the only common law of international negotiation.

Relations between States

States, like living organisms, compete to control their environment and its resources, and to wrest advantage from one another. This competition causes them to seek to join the strength of others to their own and leads to cooperation among them. Both competition and the cooperation it engenders require states to maintain constant contact with one another. They establish and maintain relations with one another out of this practical necessity.

Recognition

One state's recognition of another represents a judgment that it is in its interest to acknowledge the existence of that state as a sovereign, independent actor in international affairs, whether or not it in fact enjoys such autonomy. *Recognition of a state* does not necessarily extend recognition to its government.

The *recognition of a government* represents a judgment that the government in question is in effective control of its state, that it is likely to remain in control for some time, and that business with the polity it controls must therefore, as a practical matter, be conducted through it.

The purpose of recognizing a government is to secure the practical benefits of a relationship with the ruling authorities in another state. Those benefits may be in terms of an enhanced capacity to cooperate with those authorities or to compete with them. Diplomatic relations with another state allow, but do not require, the establishment of an *embassy* in its capital. An embassy is the entourage of a resident ambassador or chargé d'affaires. The presence of an embassy affords the sending state an opportunity directly to shape the decisions and actions of the receiving state, to gain insight into its policies and intentions, and to establish access to individuals and groups who influence it, including those at odds with its government.

If there are no practical benefits to be gained from understanding, influencing, or dealing with the government of the state in question, or if it is unlikely long to remain in power, recognition of it is mainly a symbolic act, undertaken for political effect. Recognition may also be withheld for political effect. There may be advantages to delaying recognition of a new government: to obtain its firm and credible commitment to respect specific commitments of its predecessors, or to gain something else of value from it or its allies. Nevertheless, if there are practical benefits to be gained from dealing with a government likely to remain in power, withholding recognition of it is too costly to be sustainable for long. Recognition is therefore a bargaining tool of very limited utility.

Consular and Diplomatic Relations

States establish *diplomatic relations* to manage official interaction with national governments. Diplomatic relations are the means by which states concert purposes and arrange cooperation; they are also the means by which they argue and contend with each other in nonviolent ways. Consular relations are distinct from but implicit in diplomatic relations. States establish *consular relations* to protect the interests of their citizens abroad, to promote commerce, to facilitate cultural exchange and travel, and to collect intelligence relevant to these and other matters of interest to them. Consulates may be opened to deal with these matters in part of a foreign state rather than in its entirety.

Consular relations rest on de facto recognition; diplomatic relations signify de jure recognition of governments. Neither form of relations confers a compliment on the government with whom it is established or implies approval of that government's policies and practices. Consular and diplomatic relations are simply a convenience to those who establish and maintain them, reflecting their awareness of the reality that another government controls or influences matters of interest and concern to them.

When relations between peoples are close, diplomatic relations set the framework for their daily interaction but play a relatively minor role in it. When relations are distant or strained, diplomatic representation is most useful. A diplomatic presence then provides an indispensable source of insight into the official attitudes, reasoning, and policies of the host nation. It furnishes a secure channel of face-to-face communication with decision makers and a direct means of influencing them, as well as the elites who set the limits of what is possible for them. Diplomatic exchanges reduce the likelihood of miscalculation by both sides. They hold open the possibility of a peaceful resolution of the differences between them.

States have a particular interest in informing themselves about the military capabilities and intentions of other states. If a state is an ally or potential partner, such intelligence is needed to estimate its ability to defend itself without foreign assistance or to contribute to joint operations. If it is a potential enemy, accurate reporting is required to estimate the threat it poses. States also need to communicate with each other on specialized military affairs, including dialogue and exchanges of intelligence about military matters of common concern, as well as the management of military visits and programs of cooperation. The assignment of *military attachés* serves these purposes. Such attachés are military diplomats, part of an embassy but able to approach military leaders as fellow professionals. Their credibility as spokesmen and their insights can be indispensable during wars, crises, times of tension, or when military regimes come to power.

Breaking Relations

Defiance from another government invites its censure. Those who do not understand that diplomatic relations are an instrument of statecraft rather than a stamp of approval may then call for such relations to be broken off in order to convey a symbolic rebuke to objectionable policies and practices. Unless the government breaking off relations intends to resolve its differences with the other on the battlefield, this is unwise. Even then, it is a questionable decision.

A break in diplomatic relations leaves both sides without the unique intelligence and ease of communication that these relations provide. Almost invariably, the parties find themselves compelled to devise substitutes for what they have forgone. These substitutes are seldom as direct, efficient, secure, and reliable as resident ambassadors and embassies. The settlement of differences and conflict between the contending states becomes that much more difficult. The costs of suspending direct contacts usually outweigh the benefits of its symbolic expression of disapproval. When confrontation is protracted, governments may find themselves in the awkward position of having to negotiate the reestablishment of relations with little or nothing to show for having broken them. Even in times of armed conflict, therefore, it is wise to maintain some level of relations. The only circumstance in which a break is clearly justified is when the essential security of an embassy and its personnel cannot be guaranteed by the government of its host nation.

Embassies and Their Hosts

Diplomats are exchanged between states. They are both guests and hostages of the governments to whose capitals they are assigned. Embassies must take every precaution against penetration and the theft of their secrets by their host government or third parties. They are, however, sanctuaries, not fortresses. They cannot withstand siege or armed assault by their host government or the populace of its capital. They must operate under the protection of their hosts, or not at all. Embassies that must plan for their own military defense no longer enjoy the privileges and immunities essential to their status and functioning as embassies. If its host government will not protect an embassy and its personnel or is incapable of doing so, an embassy should be withdrawn.

A wise government will treat the diplomats accredited to it well and protect them from harm. It will then be able to demand that foreign governments do the same for its diplomats. Such a government will take the initiative to court resident diplomats' good opinion of it and its nation. It will seek to incline resident diplomats to advocate cooperation and compromise when differences arise between it and their governments.

Such a government will work to ensure that diplomats who have been assigned to it are advocates of good relations upon their return to their own capitals. It will approach them to ensure that its views and policies are understood with sympathy by their governments. These results do not come automatically; they require systematic effort. Every nation likes to imagine that it is naturally charming. A few nations may, like a few individuals, in fact exercise effortless attraction for others. Most, however, do not. Nations, like individuals, innately beautiful or not, are most alluring when they work at displaying their best side and signaling their approachability to others.

The Level of Relations

Ambassadors represent their chief of state and are empowered to speak authoritatively for their chief of government. At the outset of their duties, they are received by the foreign minister and chief of state to which they are accredited. They enjoy a presumption that they will be given access to the most senior decision makers of their host government. Diplomats of lesser rank are generally afforded access at lower levels.

The withdrawal of an ambassador symbolizes a decision not to deal directly with the highest decision makers of another state but to use other means to influence them. A government considering lowering the level of its diplomatic relations with another state by withdrawing its ambassador must consider what other means it has at its disposal to influence the decisions of

97

the government of that state, and whether these means are likely to be as effective without the ability to communicate directly with the most senior levels of that government. It must also consider how it will reestablish such communication when it becomes necessary or desirable to do so.

In the absence of an ambassador, an embassy is entrusted to a *chargé d'affaires* (or, when the absence is temporary, a *chargé d'affaires ad interim*). Able as a chargé may be, he is not an ambassador. He is received not by the chief of state but by the foreign minister. Lacking the political stature of an ambassador, a chargé is less able to use discretion in the manner in which he executes instructions or to question potentially counterproductive instructions from his capital. Dialogue and other interaction between the two capitals become more rigid and less productive as a result. A chargé is less able to bluntly report politically unpalatable news to his government or to make policy recommendations to it. As a consequence, his government's policy is likely to be less empathetic and nuanced. It is therefore less likely to achieve the results it seeks.

For these reasons, if it is necessary to downgrade relations, it is often more advantageous to recall an ambassador for consultations of indefinite duration than to withdraw him formally. Relations at the ambassadorial level are thus suspended in practice rather than being terminated. Such a recall reduces the issue of a resumption of dialogue with the most senior levels of another government to one of timing. It retains the initiative and makes the resumption of such dialogue a matter of convenience rather than of negotiated formality.

THE USE OF DIPLOMATS

Diplomats are the servants of peaceable statecraft. Their work is to manage relations between states and to contain or resolve disputes between them by measures short of war. Diplomats carry messages for statesmen and negotiate on their behalf with the governments of other states. Diplomats help statesmen understand and manipulate foreign states and peoples. They counsel statesmen as they consider how best to achieve the results they seek from other states. The wise use of diplomats is a key to the successful conduct of foreign relations.

Messages and Messengers

From the earliest days, diplomats have been confidential messengers between sovereigns. The messages they convey may be oral or written. They may be intended to persuade or merely to inform; aimed at achieving results or merely at demonstrating concern about the matter they address. They may be peremptory or humble, harsh or conciliatory, imbued with empathy or with indifference to the perspectives and interests of their recipients. They may be delivered only in the capital of the recipient or in the capitals of both the sending and receiving state. They may be anonymous, delivered on behalf of a government, or personal, imbued with the prestige of a head of government.

The faithful carriage between governments of such messages and of the replies they evoke is delicate, difficult, and sometimes risky work. Those who send a message are naturally inclined to blame the diplomat to whom they entrusted it for results at odds with those they anticipated. The resentment of recipients at an unwelcome message is nearly as likely to be directed at the messenger as it is at the contents of the message itself. The greatest utility of a diplomat to his own or the other side may, ultimately, be his availability as a scapegoat for things gone awry.

To persuade, a message must be couched in terms that appeal to the interests and prejudices of its recipient. These vary from state to state and from person to person. The interests and prejudices of other states seldom coincide with those sending the message. It is wise, therefore, to ensure that the purpose and intended results of a message are well understood by the diplomat who will deliver it, but to leave the precise manner, sequence, and phrasing of its presentation to him. An oral message is better suited to this procedure than one in writing, though a brief written message can serve as the authoritative summary of the main points of a more extensive oral presentation. What is written is not easily disavowed. The remarks of a diplomat arguing for acceptance of a proposal can, however, be repudiated. This is one reason that diplomacy is more a spoken than a written craft.

A diplomat who is resident in a foreign capital deals daily with the government of the receiving state. He can present a message without provoking the attention that a special emissary would attract. Such a diplomat can provide a private means of communication between leaders that leaves no record in official channels. That is why, when secrecy or discretion is desired, it is preferable to entrust messages to resident ambassadors. When the delivery of a message is itself a message to a third party, it may be advisable publicly to recall an ambassador to his capital to receive it personally and to carry it visibly back with him to his post of assignment, or to use a special envoy.

Negotiators

The selection of those who will negotiate for them with foreign states is among the most important decisions statesmen must make. Negotiation is the reciprocal adjustment of differences. It entails compromise. Compromise is mutual sacrifice in the hope of common gain. This is a weighty matter for a state. Negotiation can narrow disputes and craft a mutually acceptable outcome from them. It can still quarrels and replace conflict with collaboration. Those who practice this art must hold firm to their own side's interests and views while finding common ground on which to build bridges to the interests and views of the other side.

Much skill is demanded of negotiators under any circumstances. International negotiation demands the highest levels of knowledge and skill of those charged with it. Negotiators between states must reach across differing historical experiences, political and economic systems, languages, and cultures to be able to resolve disputes. These are the professional skills of diplomats. When nondiplomats are selected as negotiators, it is wise to ensure that they are assisted by those with appropriate diplomatic skills, experience, and expertise.

The relatively low visibility of resident ambassadors makes them the logical choice as negotiators when it is desirable to keep negotiations out of public view as much as possible or when discussions are likely to be protracted. Ambassadors resident abroad are, however, far from their capital and its politics. It is wise to bring them home for consultations before entrusting them with the conduct of negotiations on politically complex or controversial manners.

If possible, ambassadors should be invited to participate in the crafting of negotiating instructions, whether or not they will conduct the negotiations. This can help to avoid instructions or approaches that are unrealistic or counterproductive in terms of foreign realities, however logical and persuasive they may seem at home. It will also ensure that ambassadors have the necessary insight into all relevant views in their capital, that they fully understand their state's objectives (including its hidden objectives), and that they are able to distinguish clearly between acceptable and unacceptable negotiating outcomes. The same considerations apply to embassy officials below the level of ambassador who may be charged with conducting negotiations on lesser matters or with providing essential support to a specialized negotiating team from the capital.

Special envoys may be necessary when the subject matter of a negotiation is highly technical, represents a radical shift in policy, or is of such scope and weight as to exceed the capacity of a resident ambassador or when there is no ambassador in place. When the issues are fundamental, secrecy is generally desirable. Secrecy can minimize the risk of embarrassment, should a high-level emissary fail to achieve success. The public dispatch of such emissaries may, however, be desirable when one state wishes to imbue its dealings with another with special drama.

Statesmen should pause to reflect before dispatching political figures or persons with aspirations for political prominence to negotiate on their behalf with foreign states. Such representatives can often deliver domestic political support for the agreements they conclude. Politicians are, however, naturally concerned above all with bolstering their own image at home. This may lead them either to seek a hasty success on less advantageous terms than might have been obtained with greater patience or to pursue counterproductive tactics of public confrontation if they judge that quick success may elude them. Similarly, politicians, including ministers of government, tend to invest whatever they have negotiated with their personal prestige. This can make bad bargains more difficult to undo.

Decision makers should seldom attempt to conduct negotiations themselves. Negotiation by their subordinates can be *ad referendum*. Decision makers then have time for final review of what has been agreed. Such review allows second thoughts by decision makers, emphasizes their authority to approve or disapprove agreements, maximizes their freedom to interpret what has been agreed, and lessens the probability that later differences of interpretation will have to be referred directly to them for resolution.

Meetings at the level of chief of government are meetings between personages who are both politicians and the ultimate decision makers for their states. Such "summit meetings" are motivated more by the domestic politics of the participants than by the issues they discuss. Success is commonly measured in terms of political benefits to leaders rather than in the changes they can broker in relations between states. High-level meetings put great pressure on both sides to reach agreements for which their leaders can claim political credit. They therefore require meticulous planning and prenegotiation of their outcomes. A leader eager for the prestige of a meeting with a foreign counterpart will often authorize concessions in negotiations beyond those that would normally be made. High-level meetings can give useful impetus to negotiations.

The drive to produce documents for their principals to ratify can, however, rush negotiators into needless compromises and the conclusion of empty or unimplementable agreements. In negotiation, pressure to produce a result to adorn a political event can dull judgment, weaken resolve, and lead to concessions that prove unsustainable. Haste begets imprecision, which then waits in ambush to harass and impede the implementation of what had seemed to be agreed. Differences over the interpretation of agreements may build rancor rather than confidence between the parties to them.

When national leaders meet, the court of last resort is in session. What is decided directly between them, however mistaken, imprecise, or unimplementable it may be, cannot be disavowed without embarrassment to them. It is therefore best not to schedule summit meetings until their success has been fully prepared and ensured by lower-level negotiators. Such meetings should generally ratify, not make, agreements.

Expertise on Foreign States and Societies

Agreements between states are compacts between parties with different cultures and expectations, often written in different languages. They are interpreted and implemented by consensus of the parties rather than by reference to a third party or higher authority. The durability of agreements rests on the extent to which those who negotiated them have reached across the barriers of culture and language to forge a common understanding of what is to be done. Such understanding comes from empathy born of extended dialogue, mutual familiarity, and a common grasp of detail. Diplomats are dedicated to the development of such relationships between themselves and the states they represent. Their use as negotiators, or to support negotiators, can make a unique contribution to the success of negotiations, as well as to the implementation of the agreements they produce.

The expertise of diplomats about foreign governments and societies differs from that of scholars. Diplomacy is applied social science; it is political, economic, and cultural engineering that focuses on practical results. Scholars seek to understand foreign nations; diplomats strive to anticipate and shape their decisions. This expertise is a unique resource for statesmen as they try to alter the perceptions and calculations of foreign states to serve the interests and objectives of their own.

All experts are quicker to see the complexities of problems than the paths to their solution. Diplomats, like other experts, are prone to dwell on the reasons that something may not be accomplishable rather than to focus on how it can be achieved. The best diplomats are those who can set aside their natural caution and pessimism to help statesmen craft policies and take actions that will overcome obstacles and reach the results they seek, despite the complexities of doing so. Statesmen who make the effort to identify diplomats capable of such ingenuity and to lead them in solving problems will greatly improve the prospects for the success of their statecraft.

THE SKILLS OF THE DIPLOMAT

TASKS AND SKILLS OF DIPLOMACY

Diplomats are agents, advocates, informants, and counselors of their governments, which look to them as stewards of their nations' interests abroad. There are ten unchanging principal functions of the profession of diplomacy. The international situation gives these content but does not alter their contours. Diplomats discharge these duties on their own or, sometimes, in collaboration with members of the allied professions of arms and espionage.

The major tasks of diplomats are (1) linkage of their government's decision makers to foreign counterparts; (2) advocacy of their government's policies and views; (3) negotiation on their government's behalf; (4) commendation to their government of ways to advance or defend its interests; (5) promotion of trade and investment; (6) protection of compatriots; (7) management of programs of cooperation between governments; (8) reporting and analysis of relevant local developments and realities; (9) establishment of facilitative relationships with officials and members of the elites who influence them; and (10) cultivation of an image for their nation favorable to its interests.

These ten functions are inseparably connected.

When decision makers have positive feelings toward a foreign nation they are more receptive to approaches from both its officials and businesspeople. They are also more inclined to give weight to its interests and views. When diplomats have access to a wide range of influential people, their understanding of local trends and developments is enhanced. So, then, through their reporting, is that of their government. When programs of official cooperation are well conducted, they facilitate access to those in authority and predispose them to cooperate. When diplomats' relations with such men and women are easy and informed by good understanding of local affairs and mind-sets, they are better able to help their citizens do business and to protect those who fall afoul of local law and custom.

When these tasks are properly performed, diplomats have the insight necessary to draw up plans of action to further the interests of their country. Their government will be well informed enough to be able to form its policies wisely. Diplomats will know how to present their government's positions in terms appealing to local interests and sensibilities. They will be more able to persuade host government officials to conclude agreements favorable to their country's interests. They will know how to enable effective communication between their head of government and cabinet members and corresponding officials in their country of assignment. They will be equipped to provide uniquely valuable counsel and support to direct dialogue between such officials.

The basic skills required for diplomats to carry out these tasks are in all times and places the same. Some derive from natural talent but most are acquired only through professional training and experience. These skills are mutually supportive and fall into five broadly related categories: agency, advocacy, reporting, counseling, and stewardship.

Agency

As agents of their government, diplomats must cultivate (1) mastery of the arts of negotiation; (2) a demonstrated capacity to elicit prompt, authoritative responses from their own government to the views of their host nation; (3) the ability to add the appearance of sincere personal conviction to the messages they communicate; (4) precision of expression both in their own and in other languages; and (5) a sophisticated grounding in their own nation's history and culture.

Advocacy

As advocates of their nation's policies and perspectives, diplomats must embody (1) the credibility that comes from intelligent commitment to its interests and the policies derived from them; (2) a gift for political calculation; (3) tact; (4) the empathy and ability to help their host nation redefine its interests to be compatible with those of their own government; (5) fluency in the dominant language of their host nation and the principal diplomatic language of its capital; and (6) affability and poise that shrugs at adversity.

Reporting

As reporters, diplomats must personify (1) acuity of observation and accuracy of memory; (2) discretion; (3) graceful adaptability to life in alien cultures; (4) ease of fellowship with a wide range of individuals and groups such that they readily share confidences; and (5) facility as tersely vivid but scrupulously accurate writers.

Counseling

As counselors of their own governments, diplomats must cultivate (1) a reputation for selfless dedication to their nation's interests; (2) knowledge of their host nation's history, including the record of its relations with their own country; (3) a finely honed sense of how policy is made in their own government; (4) the acumen to judge when and how to present to their government recommendations for altered courses of action or requests for new instructions; and (5) the knack of allowing others to take credit for notable policy innovation or success.

Stewardship

As stewards of their people's interests and reputation in foreign lands, diplomats must evidence (1) concern about their compatriots and a dedication to serving them; (2) understanding of commerce and finance; (3) appreciation of the essentials of military science; and (4) knowledge of diplomatic practices and international law.

These twenty-five basic skills of the diplomatic profession are born of tutoring by senior members of the profession. They are perfected through experience in carrying out professional duties. When diplomats come to possess these skills in adequate measure, they are able to perform the functions that their state expects of them.

AGENCY

Diplomats act as agents of their state in other states and in organizations created by states. They negotiate on behalf of their government with the foreign government or organization that is their host. They are responsible for explaining their government's views, as authoritatively, precisely, and persuasively as possible, to their hosts. Diplomats personify both their nation's traditions and its contemporary culture to the officials and people where they are assigned.

These responsibilities give diplomats their status under international law and in the eyes of their hosts. Professional skill in conducting the duties of agency vis-à-vis foreigners distinguishes diplomats from other foreign policy experts and analysts.

The role of agent requires the subordination of personal interests to those of the principal being represented. This requires great self-control. Agency resembles acting in that those who engage in it must present the words and convictions of others as their own. Unlike actors, however, agents improvise their script as they interact with those they are seeking to persuade. Their object is not to impress onlookers but to gain the confidence of their interlocutors so as to craft the outcomes desired by their principal. Nor should an agent seek public acclaim. Credit for success should go to the agent's principal. An agent should, however, accept blame for failure. Such aid and avoidance of harm to a principal's reputation are part of the service an agent renders to a principal.

The result sought by an agent negotiating for his principal may be understanding or agreement on particular terms for cooperation or dispute resolution. It may be delay or—less commonly—impasse or provocation. Such seeming failures can gain time for, or justify, unilateral action that an agent's principal wishes to carry out.

To achieve the results sought by his principal, an agent must be intimately familiar with his principal's objectives. He must understand the interests and presuppositions from which these objectives derive. He must possess dispassionate comprehension of the interests, predispositions, and aspirations of those he is seeking to influence. An agent must wield language with uncommon exactitude. Such precision is needed to achieve desired effects on the other side, to communicate accurately, and to avoid inadvertent misimpressions.

Diplomacy embraces these general demands for effective performance of agency. It adds to them the special requirements of international and intercultural communication. Empathy with foreign interlocutors presupposes understanding of their nation's history, culture, and mode of discourse. Verification that communication is precise requires knowledge of their language. A diplomatic agent must have a sophisticated grounding in the history and culture of his own nation. This is necessary to help his foreign interlocutors understand and accept the validity of the viewpoint of the state he is representing.

Confidentiality and discretion are as essential to the success of negotiations on matters of public concern as they are to the success of private dealings between individuals. Meetings conducted one-on-one allow a degree of candor that larger assemblies preclude. It is more difficult to retreat from a position that has been stated in the presence of others than to do so from one conveyed in private. Public articulation of a negotiating position entrenches it. Description of negotiating positions in terms of general objectives, rather than in detail, preserves flexibility.

Diplomatic agents are engaged in the public business of their nation. They must be adept at dealing with the publics and news media of their own country, as well as those of foreign countries. The crafting of public impressions is part of the negotiating process; it sets the context and influences the agenda for discussion between governments. Accomplishing this is a specialized skill of public diplomacy.

Many demands that are judged unreasonable at first hearing come to seem more acceptable when heard many times. Unembarrassed repetition of negotiating positions is part of the art of diplomatic defense. A diplomatic agent should restrain the impulse to say something original unless he intends to signal a change in his government's position. A change in position is best communicated by the omission of terms previously insisted upon rather than by their explicit modification or abandonment. Diplomats know that they must listen to what is not said as much as to what is said.

Revelation or exaggeration of selected details of the other side's position can make the other side seem unreasonable to its own public and to the diplomat's own. This can add to the pressure on the other side to clarify its position, and thus to compromise, while strengthening public backing for the diplomat's own position. Such pressure is most effective if voiced by a third party or anonymously, through leaks to the media. This avoids tainting the reputation of negotiators. If the positions being revealed or misdescribed resonate with the views of the other side's public, however, the other side's flexibility may suffer as pressure mounts on it to escalate its demands.

The choreography of meetings between principals is one of the main tasks of agency. The purpose of meetings at authoritative levels is to enhance mutual confidence and to dramatize the importance of relationships. This requires that the two sides preconcert a common agenda and sequence of events. The avoidance of surprise confirms the existence of mutual understanding and prevents embarrassment to either party. It is the responsibility of an agent to ensure that the other side is prepared to discuss the issues his principal will raise.

When principals negotiate directly, their commitments— even those conceived in haste or confusion—engage their personal prestige and mutual credibility. Leaders cannot easily disavow what they themselves have said to each other. Disagreements between principals have a finality that discord between their agents does not. Meetings between heads of state or government are therefore best devoted to the ratification of agreements prepared by their agents rather than to the negotiation of such agreements. Meetings at the summit should confirm the course that has been traveled. Leaders should point to the next destination to be attained. They must provide direction to the subordinates who must survey and build the road by which both sides will reach that destination.

Agreement on how both sides will characterize what has been discussed is the final, essential item of business in any meeting of interest to parties not represented there. The achievements of any meeting will be rapidly undone by subsequent public discord about the extent of common ground or disagreement between the parties. Efforts to inflate the importance of meetings or to exaggerate their accomplishments seldom succeed for long. Such embellishment of the facts gains momentary advantage, but risks ultimate embarrassment. It is likely to be refuted by the subsequent course of events, if not by the statements of the other party.

ADVOCACY

Like lawyers, diplomats are advocates. Both are charged with advocating and thereby advancing the interests and viewpoints of a client. In the case of lawyers, the client is whoever hires them to represent him. For diplomats, the client is the state and government they serve.

Lawyers are expected to make a client's case appear the better cause in court or in negotiations, so that it may prevail, regardless of their own opinion or evaluation of it. Their professional ethic requires them to advance their client's interests to the best of their ability consistent with the law. It is their duty to their client to counsel him how best to achieve his ends, to protect his confidences, and to urge his case while concealing any personal doubts they may have about it. These are duties their status and responsibilities as agents and advocates in a lawyer-client relationship forbid them to shirk.

So too with diplomats. They also have a professional duty to advise their government how best to advance its interests while keeping both its internal deliberations and their counsel to it in utmost confidence. This duty is the more exacting because a diplomat's opponent is another government. Its intelligence agencies and media are unconstrained in efforts to penetrate this confidentiality, whether in the diplomat's capital or in its own. A foreign government can reasonably expect loyal assistance from its citizenry. It may be supported by allies and auxiliaries. All these factors magnify the risk that a diplomat's indiscretions will come to the opponent government's attention, benefiting its cause at the expense of his own government and people.

Similarly, diplomats must do their utmost to urge their government's views and positions on other governments and peoples, regardless of their personal opinions or evaluations of these views and positions. This requires more than skill in dealing with the news media, though that is, of course, essential. Everything that diplomats write and speak, even to intimates and in the privacy of their offices and residences, must be assumed to be accessible to the other side. Diplomats therefore have a duty unwaveringly to confirm their government's stance and its merits both in public and in private.

Diplomats known personally to differ with the positions they are nonetheless advocating on behalf of their government may gain sympathy, but they will forfeit credibility. They will thereby damage their utility as advocates and injure their government's cause. So, asked even by close friends to state their own views, diplomats are bound to portray their government's position as their own and to restate it as such as convincingly as possible. (Professional colleagues and kind friends, understanding this, will ask a diplomat for his interpretation of the forces and reasoning behind his government's stand rather than for his personal views of the issue in dispute.) The position of trust in which diplomats have been placed by their government as the advocate of their people's interests and concerns demands no less of them.

The context in which diplomats operate thus sets up a standard of professional ethics more demanding of them personally than that expected of lawyers. Lawyers do their advocacy in a world divided relatively clearly between realms of public, professional activity and private life. This division, if it exists at all, is far less clear for diplomats. They act as advocates in arenas more varied and less structured than the law courts or the negotiating table.

The ethics of diplomatic advocacy reflect this diversity of contexts. They are correspondingly more complex than those the legal profession has evolved for its members. This complexity, together with the inherent difficulty of codifying standards for a transnational profession practiced under no single

116

national authority or political culture, is why they have yet to be reduced to writing.

Legal ethics are imposed and enforced by the law courts (of which lawyers are officers) or by agencies and associations operating under the authority of the courts. In cases of severe ethical lapse, lawyers may be jailed or formally barred from the practice of their profession.

No such structures or procedures exist to impose and enforce diplomatic ethics. They are imposed and enforced instead by the practical consequences that accrue to those who violate them. These consequences embrace being declared persona non grata. They include disgrace and loss of credibility and access to interlocutors, to the point of becoming ineffectual. They may entail humiliating professional and personal failure on matters that touch the life of the nation a diplomat serves. Most of all, however, they involve loss or severe damage to the trust between nations that it is the aim of the diplomatic profession to foster. Diplomats seek to foster such trust as essential to the core purpose of their profession. This purpose is to promote and facilitate negotiated rather than violent solutions to international problems.

The ethical standard to which diplomats are held in their advocacy of their government's cause derives from this professional imperative to enlarge trust and confidence between nations, as well as from the cumulative history of dealings between the states party to a particular negotiation. When such interaction has been straightforward, faithful, and without prevarication or equivocation, all sides are reasonably entitled to expect that it will continue to be so. Deviation from this standard through misleading statements or lies by a diplomat then constitutes a breach of professional ethics. It will violate the reasonable expectations of the other side, producing a loss of trust that may well be irremediable. It will evoke outrage and make the resolution of future differences far more difficult.

Conversely, when the interaction between nations has been characterized by a pattern of duplicity, lamentable as this is, its persistence violates no expectations and causes no injury worthy of outrage. No loss of existing trust can occur when dishonesty, rather than good faith, is anticipated and that expectation is then fulfilled. Nevertheless, an opportunity to enhance mutual confidence and thereby ease the resolution of future problems between the parties to the dispute will have been lost. Evidence of duplicity will be used to rally the emotions of others in the nation that has been deceived. A reputation for dishonesty is likely to increase the obduracy of opponents while reducing their willingness to risk reliance on the word of a diplomat's government in future agreements. For these reasons, diplomats always strive to raise the level of honesty and good faith in international relations.

Diplomats' primary interlocutors are, of course, the executive authorities of the governments to which they are accredited. These authorities have the responsibility to manage the international relations of the state and negotiate with foreign nations on its behalf. Yet, in doing so, they reflect the views and advocate the interests of many other individuals and institutions in their government and society. To succeed, diplomatic advocacy must reach beyond its primary interlocutors to persuade others with an influential interest in the issue, including those who form the broad opinions of their political culture. This involves, among other activities, a constant dialogue with key personalities in the local news media.

Effective advocacy requires reduction of complex issues to their factual and logical essence, defined and articulated in terms that engage the interests and emotions of the other side. This, in turn, depends on careful analysis of these interests and emotions as well as understanding of the mode of reasoning most congenial to those holding them. Arguments based on appeal to the interests and emotions of a diplomat's own countrymen, rather than his hosts, are more likely to bore, puzzle, or antagonize than to persuade. Similarly, arguments framed in terms familiar to the diplomat's intellectual culture, but alien to that of his hosts, invite dismissal as incomprehensible, self-serving, or illogical.

The objective of diplomatic advocacy is to persuade the relevant authorities of other nations either that they should do something that the diplomats' government wants them to do or that they should not do something it does not want them to do. Advocacy is therefore normally directed first and foremost at those institutions and individuals who will recommend a course of action and those who must approve it, implement it, or acquiesce in it for it to be effective. Diplomats must identify these institutions and individuals in the host government and focus their efforts at persuading them. Often the best approach will be direct, but this is not always the case.

Sometimes a single department of government, such as a ministry of foreign affairs, has full powers to do this work. More often, however, still other departments enjoy decisive influence over their government's position on the specific subject matter. Rivalry among ministers and government departments often reflects vested interests distinct from those of society as a whole. Such rivalry complicates decision making but may also provide the key to producing favorable decisions.

Diplomats must therefore seek ways to ensure that their government's viewpoint is effectively stated to the key officials of other interested or influential departments, even as they deal formally with the ministry that has been designated to deal with them. They may do this directly through office calls or informal discussion in social settings arranged by them or third parties. When such access is difficult or impossible, however, they must resort to indirect means. They may contrive direct contact between officials of counterpart ministries in their own government and those of their host government. They may also use third parties to get their case across, including nationals of their host state with long-standing relationships and superior access to specific officials who have an interest in the specific issue.

In democratic societies, it is considered a normal part of the political process for parties at interest to reach beyond the executive departments of government directly or indirectly to influence key members and elements of the legislature in a position to advance or thwart a policy decision. This game of influence, openly played or not, is, in fact, crucial to the success of policy advocacy in all political systems. If a diplomat fails to effectively advocate his cause as required for success in the political system of his host nation, and as his opponents in it will certainly urge the opposing case, he can hardly be surprised when success eludes him.

Nevertheless, the open engagement of diplomats in the rough and tumble of their hosts' internal deliberations and policy process is likely to be counterproductive, even in societies where decision making is relatively transparent. It may evoke rebuke or xenophobic resentment as foreign interference in domestic affairs. It risks focusing attention on the interests of the diplomats' nation rather than those of the host nation. This is more likely to raise suspicion than to persuade.

These indirect aspects of diplomatic advocacy must therefore be conducted subtly and discreetly, relying on individuals and groups within the host nation who share an interest in the course of action the diplomat is espousing and who can therefore act legitimately as surrogate advocates for him. They may benefit immensely from access to the resources of a foreign government that shares their objective. This assistance can provide them with a source of data and argumentation superior to any they might otherwise have. It can help to stimulate improved coordination and exchanges of information between groups that otherwise might not cooperate effectively. It can provide them with a foreign government's best and most timely information about their own government's policy debate, enabling them to target their efforts at persuasion more precisely and effectively.

Cooperation with such surrogate advocates in a diplomat's host nation is also likely to greatly enhance his understanding of the problems his cause confronts. It can improve the targeting, timing, and substance of his own official and direct advocacy of his government's position to key officials of his host government. It can ensure that his host government has multiple sources of accurate information about his government's reasoning and intentions.

For all these reasons, the enlistment of such support within the host nation is a major task of diplomacy.

DIPLOMATIC DIALOGUE

Diplomacy is the expression of national power in terms of tactfully intelligent suasion and peaceable coercion. Diplomatic persuasion is the art of convincing other states that their interests are best served by taking actions favorable to the interests of one's own state. Its principal instrument is dialogue.

Diplomatic dialogue consists of exchanges of assessments, estimates, apprehensions, preferences, options, intentions, commitments, reassurances, and verifications. Its purpose is to reach a common assessment of a situation or trend, to estimate its effects on each side's interests, to identify interests that are shared, to affirm preferences for particular outcomes, to discuss options for achieving these outcomes, to clarify intentions, to enable joint or parallel actions to achieve agreed results, and to manage such collaboration. Each step in this process is a prerequisite for the next.

Candid exchange of *assessments* of a situation or trend of concern is essential to identify the extent to which the parties' views of the situation and the factors shaping it overlap or differ. Such an exchange of analyses enriches and influences the views of both sides. It establishes a measure of mutual confidence in the seriousness of purpose of the parties even when differences exist between them.

Once the parties have determined the extent to which they agree on the nature of a situation or trend, they can exchange *estimates* of the probable consequences of the situation or trend for their respective interests. Such exchanges demonstrate awareness by each side of the interests of the other.

They build mutual respect and demonstrate the possibility of agreement.

When the parties understand the extent to which they would both gain or suffer from particular outcomes, they can identify common *apprehensions* about the probable impact of a situation or trend on the interests they share. They can then explore the ways in which particular outcomes might affect both their common and individual interests. Such exchanges engender a sense of shared risk and opportunity.

Discussion by the parties of the outcomes that would best (or least) serve their common and individual interests enables them to identify common *preferences*. This builds a sense of shared purpose.

When the parties agree on what they would like to achieve or prevent, they can explore *options* for reaching this result. Exchanges of views on alternative courses of action identify possibilities for joint or parallel actions by the parties. This lays the basis for cooperation between states on the matters at hand.

Affirmation by the parties of their will to take such actions defines their *intentions*. This defines the scope of their potential cooperation.

The exchange of *commitments* to take specific actions jointly or in parallel consolidates an understanding between the parties. This brings into being a coalition and constitutes coordination between them on the matters that are the subject of their understanding.

The exchange of information as coordinated actions proceed provides mutual *reassurances* that each party continues to bear in mind the interests of the other and *verifications* that each is acting in accord with the expectations it created in the other party. Such reassurance and verification enable the parties to manage their collaboration smoothly to the achievement of its ends.

Mature relationships between states rest on presuppositions created through past dialogue and interaction. The failure to revalidate these presuppositions continuously risks increasing misunderstanding and the loss of mutual confidence between states as relations and circumstances evolve. Lack of active dialogue deprives states of real knowledge of each other. It leaves intentions to be deduced by a priori reasoning and feeds suspicion. This engenders friction even between friends and undermines their ability to collaborate. Ignorance born of the absence of dialogue fosters miscalculation and perpetuates animosity between states that are adversaries. It increases the danger of fruitless conflict even as it precludes opportunities for cooperation where, notwithstanding rivalry, interests may coincide.

Precision of mutual understanding can be established only through the constant mutual reassessment that dialogue and efforts at diplomatic persuasion facilitate. Wise diplomacy is alert to change. It constantly tests its assumptions and adjusts its expectations. The failure to probe adversaries for openings can be costly to the state. The neglect of diplomatic dialogue and efforts at persuasion with friends can bring a state to base its strategy on illusion. This can be perilous.

Diplomatic dialogue is no less important when coercion must replace persuasion as the method by which a state seeks to influence the decisions of others. Such dialogue helps to form the impressions by which one state gauges the importance of an issue as seen by another and judges its resolve. It gives credibility to threats and ultimatums by allowing states to explain their reasons for attaching gravity to the issue in dispute. It allows them to clarify their terms for refraining from escalated political or economic pressure or from the use of force. It is how diplomatic bargaining maintains an opening for closure. It is the means by which the sides communicate concessions. It is the way of dispute resolution.

In the absence of diplomatic discourse, confrontation is left to take its mindless course. That is why, even when political emotion seems to underscore the advantages of ostracism and nonintercourse, states are wise to maintain dialogue with one another.

REPORTING AND ANALYSIS

Diplomats are the visible eyes and ears of their state in foreign lands. Their reporting describes and anticipates events and trends in terms of their implications for the national interests and concerns of the diplomats' state. The purpose of diplomatic reporting is to enable the state to act to shape events to its advantage or to mitigate the impact of unfavorable developments.

There are three kinds of diplomatic reporting. Factual reports of meetings, events, and data make up the official record that constitutes the memory of states. Biographical reports record the curricula vitae and assess the personalities, views, and policy effectiveness of influential foreigners. Analytical reports dissect the causes and implications of political, economic, cultural, or military developments and explain the policy responses of foreign states and peoples to these developments.

Factual reporting demands acuity of observation, alertness to detail, and accuracy of memory. Acuity of observation is born of familiarity with both subject matter and milieu. Without adequate expertise in the subject being discussed, a diplomat will not comprehend the full significance of what has been said (or not said) by each side in a meeting or be able to summarize it accurately. Fluency in the languages of both sides and familiarity with the ways in which each has phrased its views in the past are essential to grasp and record nuance. Alertness to detail is necessary to separate what is significant from what is not. Even the best stenographic skills require the supplement of a strong memory to produce a perceptive and accurate record. This kind of reporting is, in fact, best done by two people rather than one.

Biographical reporting requires an astute eye for character. It also demands the political acumen to discern the real workings of relations between individuals and groups beneath the masks of bureaucratic hierarchy and social niceties that conceal these. To gain such insights, a diplomat must establish candid personal relationships that reach beyond the role-playing characteristic of official interaction. Cultural sensitivity, affability, and a reputation for discretion are the keys to doing so. Biographical reporting is best when it is the product of a single insightful person.

The course of human events is set by the interaction of developments with personalities. Analytical reporting builds on factual and biographical reporting to explain the way things have moved and how they are likely to move in the future. Its basis is perspicacity, breadth of knowledge, skill at inductive reasoning, intuition informed by experience, and logic. Analytical reporting attempts to explain foreign realities to decision makers in a diplomat's own capital. Such officials often have no experience of these realities and find them both unpalatable and implausible. To be credible, and therefore useful, analysis must deftly overcome the political obsessions and perceptual gaps of those to whom it is addressed. This kind of reporting is best when it is a team effort.

The quality of diplomatic reporting is measured by its reliability, accuracy, candor, completeness, readability, relevance to national interests and concerns, and timeliness.

Only well-sourced information is reliable. Information must be accessed through individuals and institutions with relevant information. Having identified such sources, diplomats must cultivate relations with them that predispose them to share that information. Ease of fellowship with many individuals, such that they readily share confidences, is the key to collection of the wide range of information on which accurate reporting depends. The actual collection of information requires listening, not talking. The best reporting officers talk no more than is necessary to induce others to speak.

Only honest reporting is accurate. Diplomatic reporting rests on inductive reasoning from facts, not deduction from ideology or prejudice. Reporting that ignores the preconceptions of those to whom it is addressed lacks credibility. Reporting that panders to these prejudices is misleading. The duty of diplomats, as reporters, is to strive to ensure not only that their government is aware as early as possible of the truth of events and trends that can affect state interests and national concerns but also that it is persuaded of the reality and significance of these events and trends. Reporting officers are poised between the universe they are observing and their readers back home. They must be sensitive to both if their reporting is to have value. Thus, tact, as well as candor, is essential to diplomatic reporting.

Governments that condone candor will get it; those that don't, won't. Diplomats must alert their government to facts and the implications of these facts even when their government manifestly does not want to be alerted. They must be encouraged to do so even when their capital resentfully rejects the facts they observe or when their superiors resist analytical conclusions and predictions contrary to those desired or expected. The value of reporting and analysis is measured in the extent it informs and advises, not placates or courts, those who read it. The candor of diplomatic reporting depends on the integrity of the reporting diplomat, which in turn reflects the degree of official tolerance for the confidential expression of unconventional, nonconforming, or dissenting views.

Only secret reporting is complete. When there is no confidence that reporting officers can maintain security of information, no information will be shared with them. When reporting officers lack confidence in their judgments of individuals and events remaining privileged, they will not offer candid views to their government. Nor will diplomats then report the private remarks of influential individuals. The revelation of such opinions can damage those who voiced them, while destroying the reputation for discretion of the diplomat who reported them. The keeping of confidences is the key to gaining them.

Only well-written reports are read. Reports that remain unread might just as well not have been written. The shorter the report and the livelier its style, the more likely it is to attract attention from those with the capacity to address the problems it identifies. If the subject does not lend itself to brief treatment, a report should be preceded by a greatly abbreviated summary of its main points. Reports should be written to those who will read them, not for an abstract or anonymous audience in the capital. Logical organization persuades. Discursive writing leaves no clear impression.

Foreign ministries that provide guidance and feedback to diplomats abroad to help them concentrate their reporting on matters of current and potential national concern will glean such reporting. Diplomatic reporting originates far from decision makers. Left to guess what decisions are currently before policy officials in their capital, diplomats will often guess wrong.

Only timely reports are useful. Reports that arrive after decisions can realistically be made are of interest to those who enjoy speculating about what might have been. Such reporting has no impact on history.

COUNSEL

S tatesmen seek to gain benefits for their state or to avoid harm to it as it interacts with other states and peoples. Diplomats help statesmen craft as well as implement overt measures short of war to accomplish this. Diplomats are the counselors of statesmen in the arts of peace.

Counselors are collaborators who advise their principal on how best to serve his interests and achieve his ends. To regard their advice with favor, a principal must see his counselors as embracing his interests and ends as their own.

A principal may, however, perceive his interests only imperfectly, or confuse emotional imperatives with interests. He may therefore define his ends in ways that contradict his interests, properly considered. The first duty of counselors is to ensure that their principal accurately understands the nature of the interests that are at stake for him. Their second duty is to help their principal set objectives that will serve his interests. Both tasks require great analytical skill and even greater tact.

Everyone presumes himself to understand his own interests better than others do. This is why the role of counselor to kings and dictators is so difficult. Autocrats often equate their personal interests with those of the state they control. They are justly skeptical that any counselor can truly put their interests (or those of their state) ahead of his own. Statesmen who view themselves as holding the interests of their state in trust for its people are less likely to confuse their personal interests with those of their state. They can discuss the interests of the state more objectively and dispassionately. Such leaders are, however, no less likely to bridle at any implication that they misperceive their state's interests. Leading leaders to a clearer comprehension of their state's interests and a more effective definition of their state's objectives is a subtle endeavor that challenges the persuasive skill of the ablest diplomats.

The most acceptable counsel flatters rather than demeans the abilities of those to whom it is offered. The most persuasive counsel is that which convinces a decision maker that an idea he has embraced was his own inspiration or was, at least, stimulated by something he said. The most successful counselors are those who ensure that others who must support or implement a course of action gain credit for originating it. The longest-serving counselors are those who are most self-effacingly loyal.

Statesmen value the expertise of diplomats in part because diplomats understand and can explain the actions and motivations of foreign states. But it is difficult to explain actions and motivations without seeming to justify or sympathize with them. Diplomats easily come to be seen as too solicitous of the interests of foreign states and insufficiently devoted to the interests of their own. They must temper their remarks to preclude this perception or lose the ear of policymakers.

The purpose of diplomacy is not to understand and describe foreigners but to change their attitudes and behavior in desirable ways. Experts help statesmen understand what is happening; counselors help them define policy options to deal with it. Expertise on foreign behavior earns diplomats access to statesmen. Advice on how to counter or co-opt foreigners earns diplomats credibility as counselors.

Recommendations advance when they find a strong base of support in the policy machinery of government. They fail when they do not. Few ideas, however sensible, prevail unless championed by influential participants in the policy process. It is not enough to articulate a proposal. The right people must be enlisted to champion that proposal when the issues to which it relates are considered by policymakers. Often this requires persuading them to exchange visits with their foreign counterparts. Personal exposure to foreign problems and opportunities engenders a degree of commitment to addressing them that abstract consideration of issues from afar seldom does. The natural desire of senior officials to crown their foreign travels with concrete results stimulates bureaucracies to produce such results. This can provide an opening for the consideration of new ideas and initiatives.

Statesmen look to diplomats to alert them to foreign opportunities while they can still be seized and to foreign perils while they can still be deflected. Statesmen must, however, be concerned not only with what is feasible abroad but also with what is possible at home. Policies that do not correspond to foreign realities are feckless. Policies that find no resonance in domestic realities are stillborn. Diplomats are charged, first and foremost, with advising what is possible abroad. To be accepted by statesmen, however, their proposals must take account of what is possible at home. Diplomats who fail to strike this balance should not be surprised when their recommendations fail to gain serious consideration.

STEWARDSHIP

Every state seeks to ensure that other states and peoples bear in mind its political, cultural, economic, and military interests. A state must tend its image abroad if it is to predispose foreigners to cooperate with it and its citizens. Every state is concerned about the security and well-being of its nationals and their property abroad. Diplomats are the stewards of these interests.

The advantages of good relations with a state are seldom self-evident to the peoples and governments of other states. If foreigners do not recognize the benefits of maintaining cordial relations with another state, their decisions will slight the views of that state on issues of moment to it. Diplomats have the task of ensuring that foreigners appreciate the advantages of deference to the interests of the state and nation the diplomats represent.

To accomplish this, diplomats must advertise the gains that transactions with their own society will yield to foreign societies. They must call the attention of influential foreign publics to the opportunities that expanded interaction with the diplomats' country would bring, and, at least by implication, to the losses that contracted dealings would entail. Foreigners must be persuaded that their own interests and those of their country are much the same as the interests of the country diplomats represent.

The object of such public diplomacy is to affect foreign decisions on political, economic, and military matters. It takes as its target those who make these decisions. Policies are usually formed by complex interaction among different branches of government and social groups. Public diplomacy strives to incline individuals and groups with influence toward favorable decisions. Failing that, it seeks to neutralize their resistance to such decisions. Public diplomacy requires a sophisticated understanding of the political centers of gravity in the foreign society that is its target. It depends on the development of leverage that can reach and move these centers in favorable directions.

Such leverage may come either from fear of harm or from anticipation of favor by those it seeks to move. Collaboration born of fear is reluctant and resentful. It is less reliable than cooperation volunteered out of friendship. Friendship is a sense of mutual reliance and shared destiny based on sympathy, assistance, and expressions of regard. A sense of obligation for past favors, as well as the expectation of future benefits, sustains friendship. Diplomats are charged with making and keeping influential friends for their state in foreign lands.

Especially in their role as consuls, diplomats are also guardians and protectors of their fellow citizens in foreign lands. The state looks to its representatives abroad to promote commerce and facilitate trade and investment by its citizens there. Consuls ensure that travelers from their homeland enjoy legal protections from foreign states no less favorable than those these foreign states confer on their own citizens. They may be called upon to vouch for their fellow citizens with foreign officials. Consuls issue passports and other identity documents, serve as notaries, and administer the social services their state extends to its citizens abroad. They ensure respect for the sovereign immunities of their state's agencies and military vessels and aircraft in other states.

These responsibilities enlarge official access to foreign societies. They help to forge mutually supportive relationships between diplomats and compatriots who are abroad to pursue private interests. Relationships with compatriots multiply the sources of information and avenues of influence available to diplomats. Careful attention by a diplomat to the needs of his fellow citizens is mandated by the state. Even if it were not, it would be in a diplomat's personal interest to be solicitous about his compatriots' interests. Their view of him is likely to have more impact on his standing back home than his reputation among foreigners.

Such everyday duties of diplomats ease relations between peoples. They build mutual respect, deference, and understanding between states. These are the prerequisites for peaceable statecraft.

REASON OF STATE, SYSTEM, AND RELATIONSHIP

Diplomats are officers of the state and its agents of nonviolent interaction with other states and peoples.

The state is itself the agent of its polity, the incorporation and instrument of a people's will in their competition and cooperation with other peoples. As the agent of the nation, the state must pursue the ends the nation has assigned to it. The nation, as principal in this relationship—rather than the state, as agent—also properly determines the means by which the state may pursue these ends on the nation's behalf. No more than any other agent may the state substitute its own conscience for that of its principal. The state is an amoral entity; it is the instrument of others' moral judgments rather than the originator of its own.

Reason of State

Yet, a state is created for clear purposes: to protect the interests and realize the aspirations of the nation that created it. It must be true to these purposes. The state fulfills these purposes by acting to ensure the survival, security, well-being, domestic tranquility, strategic advantage, and other interests of its nation in the most efficacious manner it can, consistent with the means its nation has decreed to be acceptable. This is why the state exists. *Reason of state* derived from these purposes justifies its actions vis-à-vis other states and peoples, whether violent or nonviolent in nature.

The first duty of diplomats as officers of their state, taking precedence over all others, is to advance its purposes and, hence, the interests of their nation. As agents of their state, diplomats cannot substitute their own morality for that of their principal. They are bound as a matter of their profession to execute actions dictated by reasons of state.

Reason of System

The logic of the profession of diplomacy is the pursuit of negotiated change in international relations. This logic is best expressed in an international state system that enhances the prospects for the nonviolent resolution of disputes and expanded cooperation among states. Such an international order consists of norms and practices of state behavior and international legal and regulatory regimes conducive to peaceful change. The need to defend and improve international order generates a *reason of system* that is an important source of state policy as well as of professional ethics in diplomacy.

Reason of system compels a firm response to challenges to the international system from revolutionary powers and rogue leaders who seek broadly to subvert or overthrow it. Statecraft based on reason of system may take the form of diplomacy, covert action, the use of force, or all of these. It may rely on patient efforts to contain and isolate an outlaw state until it is prepared to respect the system and work within it. Such statecraft may bring economic or political pressure to bear on such a state to compel it, in time, to reconsider its stance and to change its behavior. It may lead to military or covert action to replace the outlaw government or eliminate its leadership. Statecraft based on reason of system may also take the form of actions and inducements that, over time, so entangle a revolutionary state in the benefits of the existing order that such a state loses its revolutionary zeal to overthrow that order.

The logic of diplomacy is to cement relationships between states and peoples so as to facilitate communication, amicable interaction, and cooperation between them. Diplomacy favors courses of action that open bilateral or multilateral relationships or enhance them, rather than those that foreclose such ties or detract from them. Reason of system often seems to contradict this logic. Yet, the aim of the actions dictated by reasons of system is always to foster or reestablish conditions in which diplomacy can operate normally. The second professional duty of diplomats is to act in accord with reason of system. They must act in such a way as to ensure that the functioning of the international state system is sustained and improved.

Reason of Relationship

The normal operation of diplomacy dictates efforts to buttress relations with allies and friends and to avoid severing communication or precluding rapprochement with enemies. This course sustains existing patterns of international support for a state while leaving open the possibility that it can augment these in future, as circumstances permit. It facilitates the collection of useful intelligence and enhances the prospects for the peaceable composition of differences with other states, whether such states are allies, friends, adversaries, or enemies. In feudal state systems, in particular, *reason of relationship* with a hegemonic power may assume primary importance in the statecraft and diplomacy of lesser states. Obedience to reason of relationship is the third professional duty for diplomats.

The State and the Diplomat

The way of statecraft lies in reasons of state, system, and relationship. Diplomacy, like covert action and war, is the obedient instrument of reason of state. Reasons of system and relationship are, however, its special realm. When intelligence and military officers interact with their foreign counterparts to foster the international state system or bilateral relationships, they do so in a diplomatic capacity rather than in the exercise of the central purpose of their professions. When diplomats act to enlarge the arena in which international competition can proceed without engendering violence or to enhance trust among nations, they are carrying out the core function of their profession. The professional ethic of diplomacy therefore emphasizes reasons of system and relationship over reason of state.

Unlike the states they serve (which are corporate abstractions), diplomats are human beings. They must be true not only to their professional role but also to their own conscience.

If reason of state seems to compel a course of action beyond the limits of the permissible established by national values, diplomats are bound to seek and espouse other means to achieve its ends and to advance their nation's interests. Their profession will impel them to look for inspiration in reasons of system or relationship. Nevertheless, reason of state takes precedence over all else in statecraft. The profession of diplomacy is an aspect of statecraft. For diplomats as professionals, soundly composed reason of state must outweigh all other considerations.

If the course of action dictated by reason of state is morally repugnant, professional duty and individual conscience will conflict. Diplomats cannot then avoid a choice between continued service to their state and continued allegiance to personal moral principles. Their conscience as individuals may dictate their resignation from their profession to avoid participation in implementation of the policy decision to which they object. Their final professional responsibility is to bear in mind reasons of system and relationship, as well as their loyalty to their state, as they determine the timing and manner by which they will resign. These considerations will often dictate silence where the heart argues for public protest.

INDEX

Access
  profession of diplomacy, 107
Accommodation
  diplomatic maneuver, 79
Acumen
  counsel, 109
Adaptability
  reporting, 109
Adjustment
  concessions, 75
  limited, 79
  political measures, 39
  war, 62
  war termination, 65
Advocacy, 109, 115-120
  adversary process, 120
  advocates, 115
  compatriots, 134
  credibility, 109
  diplomats, 108
  direct, 119
  effective, defined, 118
  elements, 109
  ethics, 116
  indirect, 119
  influencing the political
    climate, 118
  intelligence from foreign
    governments, 120
  intermediaries,119
  legislatures, 119

  ministries other than for-
    eign affairs, 119
  ministry of foreign affairs,
    119
  objective, 118
  open intervention in
    internal affairs, 120
  personal opinions, 116
  profession of diplomacy,
    107, 108
  surrogates, 120
  targets, 119
  third parties, 120
Advocates
  advocacy, 115
  surrogate, 120
Agency, 111-114
  advocacy, 111
  culture, national, 108
  diplomats, 137
  empathy, 109, 112
  language fluency, 109
  negotiation, 108
  object, 111
  poise, 109
  political calculation, 109
  precision, 108
  profession of diplomacy, 108
  responsiveness, 108
  sincerity, 108
  tact, 109

141

Chas. W. Freeman, Jr., has led a distinguished diplomatic career, including service overseas in India, Taiwan, the China mainland, Thailand, and Saudi Arabia. He was assistant secretary of defense for international security affairs from 1993 to 1994 and U.S. ambassador to the Kingdom of Saudi Arabia from 1989 to 1992 (during the Gulf War). Before serving in Riyadh, he had been the principal deputy assistant secretary of state for African affairs; deputy chief of mission at the U.S. embassies at Beijing and Bangkok; director of three offices in the Department of State and one in the United States Information Agency; and deputy United States coordinator for refugee affairs. He was the principal American interpreter during President Richard Nixon's historic visit to the People's Republic of China in February 1972.

Freeman attended the Universidad Nacional Autónoma de México, Yale University, and Harvard Law School. He was a senior fellow in the Jennings Randolph Program at the United States Institute of Peace in 1994–95, following his decision to retire from the United States Foreign Service. He was elected to the American Academy of Diplomacy in 1995.

Freeman is currently chairman of Projects International, Inc., a Washington-based business development firm specializing in the arrangement of joint ventures for its American and foreign clientele.

United States Institute of Peace

The United States Institute of Peace is an independent, nonpartisan federal institution created and funded by Congress to promote research, education, and training on the peaceful resolution of international conflicts. Established in 1984, the Institute meets its congressional mandate through an array of programs, including research grants, fellowships, professional training programs, conferences and workshops, library services, publications, and other educational activities. The Institute's board of directors is appointed by the President of the United States and confirmed by the Senate.

Chairman of the Board: Chester A. Crocker
Vice Chairman: Max M. Kampelman
President: Richard H. Solomon
Executive Vice President: Harriet Hentges

Board of Directors

Chester A. Crocker (Chairman), Research Professor of Diplomacy, School of Foreign Service, Georgetown University

Max M. Kampelman, Esq. (Vice Chairman), Fried, Frank, Harris, Shriver and Jacobson, Washington, D.C.

Dennis L. Bark, Senior Fellow, Hoover Institution on War, Revolution and Peace, Stanford University

Theodore M. Hesburgh, President Emeritus, University of Notre Dame

Seymour Martin Lipset, Hazel Professor of Public Policy, George Mason University

Christopher H. Phillips, former U.S. ambassador to Brunei

Mary Louise Smith, civic activist; former chairman, Republican National Committee

W. Scott Thompson, Professor of International Politics, Fletcher School of Law and Diplomacy, Tufts University

Allen Weinstein, President, Center for Democracy, Washington, D.C.

Harriet Zimmerman, Vice President, American Israel Public Affairs Committee, Washington, D.C.

Members ex officio
Ralph Earle II, Deputy Director, U.S. Arms Control and Disarmament Agency

Toby Trister Gati, Assistant Secretary of State for Intelligence and Research

Ervin J. Rokke, Lieutenant General, U.S. Air Force; President, National Defense University

Walter B. Slocombe, Under Secretary of Defense for Policy

Richard H. Solomon, President, United States Institute of Peace (nonvoting)

Jennings Randolph Program for International Peace

This book is a fine example of the work produced by senior fellows in the Jennings Randolph fellowship program of the United States Institute of Peace. As part of the statute establishing the Institute, Congress envisioned a program that would appoint "scholars and leaders of peace from the United States and abroad to pursue scholarly inquiry and other appropriate forms of communication on international peace and conflict resolution." The program was named after Senator Jennings Randolph of West Virginia, whose efforts over four decades helped to establish the Institute.

Since 1987, the Jennings Randolph Program has played a key role in the Institute's effort to build a national center of research, dialogue, and education on critical problems of conflict and peace. More than a hundred senior fellows from some thirty nations have carried out projects on the sources and nature of violent international conflict and the ways such conflict can be peacefully managed or resolved. Fellows come from a wide variety of academic and other professional backgrounds. They conduct research at the Institute and participate in the Institute's outreach activities to policymakers, the academic community, and the American public.

Each year approximately fifteen senior fellows are in residence at the Institute. Fellowship recipients are selected by the Institute's board of directors in a competitive process. For further information on the program, or to receive an application form, please contact the program staff at (202) 457-1700.

Joseph Klaits
Director

ARTS OF POWER

This book is set in Garamond Book. Hasten Design Studio designed the book's cover, and Day W. Dosch and Joan Engelhardt designed the interior. Pages were made up by Helene Y. Redmond. The book's editor was Nigel Quinney.